Grading Strategies for the College Classroom:

A Collection of Articles for Faculty

Edited by Maryellen Weimer, Ph.D.

Foreword by Barbara E. Walvoord, Ph.D.

Published by Magna Publications

Contents

Foreword

by
Barbara E. Walvoord, Ph.D.

When faculty members are asked to suggest possible workshop topics, grading is one of the most common requests. This is as true now as it was 20 or 30 years ago. No wonder, then, that grading has been a topic of enduring interest in the pages of *The Teaching Professor,* and that a collection of these articles is welcome and timely.

Most of these articles discuss how faculty members have dealt with various problems and challenges in grading. Two challenges seem prominent: how to expand what a grade measures or what it can convey, and how to deal with students who focus narrowly on grades rather on learning. Behind these challenges lies a deeper issue—the nature of the grade as a letter/number.

A grade is a letter that supposedly conveys the level of student competence. An obvious audience for a grade is external people who need a quick way to evaluate potential employees or potential students for a four-year or graduate program. Such a judgment would not be necessary in a tribal society where everyone knew everyone else. Grades are only necessary in a society where people must make quick judgments about strangers.

That itself is problematic because we, who know our students, must reduce all the complexities of a student's work into a single mark. We know what is left out. Further, when we give grades, our students are the first audience, and we are most immediately aware of the impact of the grade not on the external employer or admissions office, but on the student him/herself. Many of the articles in this collection suggest how to expand what the grade measures and conveys, and how to manage its impact on the student.

This situation would be difficult enough if letter grades would remain letters. But the letter is often translated into a number, which makes it much more powerful in our students' lives. It is that numerical quality that gives rise to many of the challenges instructors and students face, so let's think for a moment about grades as numbers.

In some classes, instructors begin with numerical scores and translate those into grades (on this test, 94–100 is an A; 86–93 is a B; and so on). On the other end, letter grades are regularly translated into numbers, thereby making it possible to calculate a GPA, to rank students (upper 10 percent of the class), and to attach descriptive words to the degree (summa cum laude).

Nowadays, when rubrics are widespread, a student's work may be assigned a score on a number of different rubric parameters—for example the thesis, evidence, citation of sources, and so on. The rubric levels may be designated by words such as "excellent," "good," and "needs work" or "exceeds expectations," "meets expectations," and "does not meet expectations," but no one is fooled. These words can be translated into letters and numbers.

Likewise,when responding to drafts or to pieces that will be collected into a portfolio, the instructor may give comments without grades, but both students and instructors are aware that certain words imply grade equivalents (e.g., "this is an excellent argument" or "this is a good start, but it needs substantial revision").

When grades are translated into numbers, they can assume powerful roles. A GPA affects many aspects of a student's life: A student must maintain a certain grade average to receive financial aid; graduate schools use grades to decide admission; employers use grades to evaluate potential employees; and a first-year student once informed me, with some chagrin, that his parents took away his car because his grade point average was too low. No wonder students are so focused on grades.

Many of the articles in this collection focus on dealing with the fact that grades are reductive judgments given by us to students who are not strangers, and that grades, with their power expanded by numeracy, have such an enormous impact on students' lives that it's difficult for students to focus on learning rather than on grades.

So, as these articles document, we try to help one another figure out how to expand the grades with comments (but how to find the time?), to evaluate the writing process as well as the product, to grade participation, to expand beyond multiple-choice questions, to grade effort, or to ensure that we are testing real learning rather than rote memorization. And we try to help one another figure out how to deal with students who focus narrowly on the grade, do not use our comments, feel a sense of entitlement, or negotiate with us for higher grades.

Every faculty member struggles with these unavoidable challenges—the reductive nature of grades, their quality as numbers, and their power in students' lives. This collection offers wisdom from the trenches—always welcome, always timely.

Chapter 1:
Grading Exams and Quizzes

Exams: Maximizing Their Learning Potential

By Maryellen Weimer, Penn State Berks, Pennsylvania

We give students exams for two reasons: First, we have a professional responsibility to verify their mastery of the material. Second, we give exams because they promote learning. Unfortunately, too often the first reason overshadows the second. We tend to take learning outcomes for granted. We assume the learning happens almost automatically, provided the student studies.

But what if we, as designers of exam experiences, consider how we might maximize the inherent potential of exams?

Review sessions—Some faculty don't have in-class review sessions because that means one less period for covering content. The question is whether students benefit more from being exposed to additional material or from having a chance to organize, summarize, distill, and integrate the content they must now learn for the exam. Should students do this summarizing and integrating on their own as they study? Perhaps. Will they learn to do it better if their efforts are guided by an expert who understands how the content domain is organized? Probably.

Typically, in the review session the teacher goes over important or challenging content. Students are supposed to ask questions, and they do, but generally they focus their questions on trying to ferret out what's going to be on the exam.

There are better alternatives. The teacher who already knows (and loves) the content doesn't need to review it. Students need to review. The period should be structured so that students are doing the work, with the teacher providing guidance. They can be working individually or in groups, but they should be solving problems, answering old exam questions, writing possible test questions, or extrapolating key concepts from assigned readings.

Groups could be given different topics, concepts, problem sets, for example, and tasked with preparing review materials/study guides for the rest of the class. They could bring these materials to the review session and present and/or distribute them.

In addition to revisiting the content and seeing more clearly how individual topics relate, review sessions can also be used to help students figure out what's going to be on the test. That's a question they shouldn't need to ask the teacher. The answer is a function of determining what's most important and how the content is going to be applied. And that's a skill students need to develop.

Exams—Regular exams don't promote deep learning because the questions don't challenge students to think. Many students memorize well; they forget with the same efficiency.

Questions that challenge students to think are much harder to write, and for that reason you don't find a lot of them in question banks that accompany textbooks. The problem is not with the multiple-choice format per se. SAT and ACT questions are multiple-choice, and many of those are quite challenging. If exams are returned to students, then new questions must be generated for each new class.

It is smarter to let students have access to their exams (when they're returned and subsequently kept in the prof's office) but not to let them keep their exams. That way, questions can be recycled, and across the years a collection can be developed, revised, and reused.

Exam circumstances rarely change. Students work alone without access to resources and under surveillance so that they don't cheat or they cheat less. This newsletter does highlight with some regularity different kinds of exam experiences—such as having the students take the exam individually and then take the same exam with a group.

Their grade may be some combination of their individual score and the group score. Or let students prepare a crib sheet (of a specified size) that they are allowed to use during the exam. Preparing a crib sheet forces students to make decisions about what's going to be on the exam.

Debrief sessions—Typically teachers go over the most-missed questions, but that approach may not be the best way to maximize the learning potential that is still present after the exam. Teachers don't need to correct the answers—students do. Whether in groups or individually, students can be given the chance to find the correct answers and fix their mistakes.

Maybe that happens during the debrief session, or maybe students do the work at home, completing it before the next class session. Maybe their grade isn't recorded until they've corrected their errors, and maybe it's a few points higher if they get all their mistakes taken care of.

Debrief sessions can also be designed so that they address some of the decisions students have made about preparing for the exam. Class attendance makes a difference. You can say that, but you should show some evidence. Take the five highest exam scores and list the number of times that group of students missed class. Take the five lowest scores and list the number of class sessions that group missed. Let the facts speak for themselves.

Many students aren't taking enough notes in class. You can say that, or you can demonstrate it. Pick a question that many people missed. Identify the date that material was covered and have everybody look at their notes. Do they have what they need there to answer the question? Were they absent and got notes from somebody else? Do they understand those notes?

Quick discussions of topics such as these can be concluded with students writing themselves a memo addressing "things I learned taking this exam that I want to remember for the next one." Collect those memos and return them shortly before the next exam.

Exams motivate students and results in learning. They review their notes, read the text, and talk with each other. The question is how much and how well they learn. How seriously they study determines part of the answer to that question. But it is also answered by the design of the exam experience, including what happens before, during, and after the event. Exam experiences can be designed so that more of their potential to promote learning is realized.

Reprinted from *The Teaching Professor*, 26. 4 (2012): 3.

The Reflective Final

By Ed Cunliff, University of Central Oklahoma, Oklahoma

Before returning to the classroom after 20-plus years in academic administration, I used to tease my spouse about all the effort she put into grading finals. From the moment they were turned in until the grades were due, she would work nonstop on grading. Why make all that effort when many students would never get to the comments if they got their semester grades first and they were what they wanted or expected? At that point they were ready to move on to whatever was next in their lives and cared little about her careful comments.

But when I went back to teaching, the joke was on me. Now I had to figure out a way to make the final and its feedback meaningful for students.

What has evolved I refer to as a "reflective final." It is a blend of several ideas and has worked well, in my estimation. Rather than students completing a final and being done with it, my students do a learning project, and we all reflect on it. Several important concepts were involved in the evolution of this final assignment.

At my institution, focus has been placed on the concepts of transformative learning, as proposed by adult educators, and high-impact programs, such as those suggested by George Kuh and others. A culminating or capstone experience has been recommended as a high-impact program.

In this approach, primarily associated with the completion of a program of study, students bring all that they've learned together in a package that makes sense to them. And that made sense to me. A final should pull the semester's experiences together into relevant closure. Self-reflection is an inherent part of what adult educators describe as transformative learning.

The question for me was how to create a final experience that would encourage this self-reflection at the same time students were pulling together what they had learned in the course.

I knew for sure the answer was not having students restate what had been discussed in class. With a background in adult education, I have been trained to think about the higher levels of Bloom's taxonomy, including the new taxonomy that puts creativity on the top level, and it is there that I found the answer.

I would challenge students to create something new that they could apply to their own life situations—a reflective final. As part of the adult education philosophy, we are always looking for ways for students to connect with their current jobs or move toward anticipated careers.

The challenge varies from class to class, but the general format is to ask for a reflection, creation, or synthesis and to allow the class to discuss each individual's product. For example, in my Educational Evaluation class the primary "text" is Donald Kirkpatrick's four-level evaluation model. A week or two before the end of the semester I introduce students to Michael Scriven's Key Evaluation Checklist. Students have until the day of the final to prepare a brief paper in which they create their own evaluation model or justify the use of Kirkpatrick's or Scriven's steps.

Usually only a few select the justification model; most create their own syntheses, and some develop something entirely unique. During the final exam period, they present and discuss their work, sometimes in small groups and sometimes to the whole class. This process helps me in the grading process. I will have heard some discussion of their work, so it's not new, and that saves time when I sit down to grade it.

The reflective final allows students to use what they've studied to create something of their own. It keeps them engaged until the last moment of the class and is different from most finals, for which they are just doing what needs to be done to get that one last grade in the course.

My assignment still isn't perfect, but I'm no longer teasing my wife. I'm appreciating the challenge of making all my students' contact with the content meaningful for them and for me.

Reprinted from *The Teaching Professor,* 26. 5 (2012): 1.

A Different Kind of Final

By Karinda Barrett, Tallahassee Community College, Florida

Last semester, I implemented a different kind of final exam. In the past I have used the standard multiple-choice and short-answer exams. I was thinking about making a change when I discovered Beyond Tests and Quizzes: Creative Assessment in the College Classroom, edited by Richard J. Mezeske and Barbara A. Mezeske.

The second chapter, "Concept Mapping: Assessing Pre-Service Teachers' Understanding and Knowledge," describes an assessment method that tests higher-level thinking. The author shared his experience using concept maps as a final exam, included an example of the final exam project, offered rubrics for grading, and discussed the advantages and disadvantages of the strategy. I decided this was the change I was going to make.

My first step was to contact the author. I did reach him, and we had a great conversation. Excited about offering this different kind of learning experience, I jumped right in, developing my own assignment and grading rubric.

On the first day of class, I told the students that they wouldn't have a final exam in the traditional sense, but they would have a final exam project. They were equally enthusiastic, but not for the right reason. They thought no final meant they didn't need to study as diligently, and consequently they didn't learn the material as well as my previous students had.

For this final my students had to construct concept maps representing their individual understanding of what they learned throughout the semester. I provided them with an article on concept mapping and gave them step-by-step directions with examples and illustrations.

The work started with students selecting a global issue, metaphor, umbrella concept, or theme. Then they decided how to format their concept maps. They could choose between a two-dimensional poster and an electronic tool such as Cmap, Visio, or other concept mapping software. The assignment challenged students to consider a wide range of issues and concepts to build their maps, including logical connectives (lines) and justi-fications (minimal phrases or guiding words). I provided questions that guided this process.

Students submitted rough drafts, and I offered feedback while there was still time for them to make changes. Once the maps were completed, stu-dents had to write 250-word explanations of their projects. They submitted the completed maps in Blackboard, including photos of the poster boards and links to electronic files.

I used a rubric with five equally weighted categories: (1) the 250-word summary explaining the concept map; (2) clear focus, logical connectives, and justifications; (3) displays of an array of subject-related concepts; (4) vi-sual appeal, clarity, and neatness; and (5) presenting in a professional man-ner. During the final exam period, each student had two minutes to present his or her concept map to the class.

The assignment encouraged student creativity, and my students took advantage of the opportunity, using many different themes and metaphors. For example, some of them used baseball, baking, and gardening as themes to express the concepts and the connections. I was impressed with their cre-ativity. This was one assignment I didn't get bored grading.

Here's what some of my students said when I asked for written feed-back on the final exam project:

- When you teach what you learned, it helps make it stick.
- The draft was helpful because it forced me to work on the project ahead of time.
- I feel that I was more challenged to know and apply the material. I liked it better than papers.
- Much better than regular exams, more fun, and assuming I did well, less pressure!

Not all their feedback was positive:

- I don't feel that I demonstrated enough. Two minutes to me was kind of short.
- This late in the semester, my creativity was tapped, and this made it difficult, where it was meant to be more fun.
- It started off slightly confusing, but once I understood what was ex-pected it was fun and enlightening.

I had to agree with the students that it was fun to do something different, and having them share what they learned with the class was a great way to wrap up the semester. I do think I did them a disservice by telling them that they wouldn't have a final exam at the end of the course. I think that affected how much they studied.

Would I use this assignment again? Definitely, but not in place of a final exam. I would use it as an alternate way to assess students' learning earlier in the course, maybe in place of a midterm exam. I would also tweak the assignment just a bit. I would give the students a set number of concepts (say, 10 or 12) to include in their maps. They definitely need more time to present. I think somewhere between five and 10 minutes would work best.

One of the things I love most about teaching is the opportunity to try something different. Once in a while these changes work perfectly, but most of the time there is room for improvement. I'm glad I tried this alternative to the final. I learned lessons that will help my students learn more effectively from the assignment next time I use it.

Reprinted from *The Teaching Professor*, 26.7 (2012): 1.

A New Way to Assess Student Learning

By Deborah Bracke, Augustana College, Illinois

I'm "reflecting" a lot these days. My tenure review is a few months away, and it's time for me to prove (in one fell swoop) that my students are learning. The complexity of this testimonial overwhelms me because in the context of the classroom experience, there are multiple sources of data and no clear-cut formula for truth.

One of the courses I teach is EDUC 340, Methods of Inclusion. The cornerstones of this 10-week class are differentiated instruction, universal design for learning, and the special education procedures/services needed to meet a variety of student needs. Embedded in this instructional blueprint are a multitude of professional teaching standards that encompass a variety of knowledge, skills, and dispositions.

My students begin the course with very little knowledge about disabilities. Therefore, in some respects, it is not too difficult to provide evidence that they have learned. So when the "rubber met the road" during my first pre-tenure review, I was able to provide more than ample evidence of student learning. Pre- and post-tests were supported with portfolio assessments, reflection papers, group projects, and the usual course evaluations. Together, these instruments assured the faculty review committee that there was a defensible connection between my teaching and students' learning.

As I prepare for my second pre-tenure review, I want to be even more deliberate and thoughtful in my assessment of teaching and learning. The retrospective pretest-post-test, developed by Campbell and Stanley in 1963, fulfilled this objective.

Unlike the traditional pre- and post-test design (where students answer questions about content on the first day of class and then answer those same questions at the end of the course), this method asks students on the last day of class to reflect and numerically indicate their level of understanding of a particular course objective when the course began and then to consider and numerically rate their understanding of that same objective at the end of the course. The difference between these two self-reported scores could be considered an index of their learning.

Identifying the most salient objectives of EDUC 340 was a daunting task, but I was able to decide on a set of 27 learning targets that addressed the core principles of the course. (An example of one of these indicators is "Students will understand the areas of exceptionality in learning as defined in the Individuals with Disabilities Education Act.") I then formatted these targets across two columns: a "Before I took EDUC 340" column and an "After I took EDUC 340" column.

I listed the 27 learning targets and asked students to consider (and calculate using a seven-point Likert scale) any perceived change in their understanding of each. The seven response options I included ranged from No Knowledge (1) to Confident Understanding (7). This scale encouraged students to think about their progress (or lack of it), and it allowed me to verify the extent to which learning had occurred.

The data this assessment generates enables me to better plan for the next class. It helps me craft assignments, build/revise content, and evaluate individual and whole-group progress. If I use the assessment regularly, I can compare different classes. I can also look at individual learning targets and correlate them with the effectiveness of specific assignments and/or teaching strategies. In effect, a retrospective pretest-post-test data set lends itself to a multitude of inquiries ultimately answering the questions "Did I help my students learn?" and if so, "What was it that they actually learned?"

Aside from its contextual relevance, this assessment is also easy and efficient to administer. It doesn't take a lot of class time, and it's a flexible format. I can add, delete, or revise the learning targets I include on the form. Similarly, if a topic emerges in a particular class, I can include it on the assessment form.

Student learning can and should be assessed in a variety of ways. So by no means am I marginalizing other end-of-course assessments or assuming a kind of simplicity that doesn't exist. There are advantages and disadvantages to any method we choose to assess learning.

What is especially valuable about assessment is the way it opens the door to our most important educational work—the work of student learning. I have found that the retrospective pre- and post-test assessment opens the door wide, and for this reason I am motivated to share it.

Reprinted from *The Teaching Professor,* 27.2 (2013): 1.

Cumulative Exams

by Maryellen Weimer, Penn State Berks, Pennsylvania

Students don't like them—that almost goes without saying. They prefer unit exams that include only material covered since the previous exam. And they'd like it even better if the final weren't a comprehensive exam but one last unit test. But students don't always prefer what research shows promotes learning and long-term retention, and that is the case with this study of the effects of cumulative exams in an introductory psychology course.

Exam performance of students in two sections of the course was analyzed. In the noncumulative section, students took three 50-question multiple-choice exams and a comprehensive final in which 55 percent of the questions covered material from across the course. In the cumulative section, students took three 50-question multiple-choice exams, but the second and third exams both included 10 questions covering material from the previous exams.

Students in this section took the same final as did those in the noncumulative section. Additionally, students in both sections took a follow-up exam two months after the course ended. That exam included 50 multiple-choice questions covering course content, and they were not questions that appeared on the exams taken during the course.

Students were also surveyed about their exam preparation, studying, and preferences. As predicted, those taking the noncumulative section were happier with the exam format than were those in the cumulative section. Other than that there were no significant differences in the students' perceptions of things such as exam difficulty, their study methods, or the number of hours they reported they spent studying for the exams.

But there were differences in their performance on the final, on chapter quizzes, and in their overall course grade. All these differences favored students in the section with cumulative exams.

The researcher also divided students in each section into low- and high-scoring groups based on the scores earned in the first exam. (College GPA could not be used to group the students, as most of them were first-semester college students.) These groupings revealed some of the most interesting findings from this study. For students in the high-scoring group, quiz grades were unaffected by section, but students in the low-scoring group of the cumulative section did better on the quizzes than did the low-scoring students in the noncumulative section. This difference was statistically and academically significant.

Low-scoring students in the cumulative section averaged a B quiz grade and those in the noncumulative section a C quiz grade. The same effect was seen in final course grades, with those in the cumulative section ending up with a B average and those in the noncumulative section with a C+ average. It emerged again in scores on the exam taken two months after the course ended.

High-scoring students' long-term retention was not affected by the experimental manipulation, but low-scoring students remembered more if they had the four cumulative exams.

The researcher explains the results this way: "Most likely, having multiple cumulative exams motivates low-scoring students to engage in behaviors that promote better performance and long-term retention. High-scoring students probably already have the motivation to engage in these types of behaviors." (p. 18)

Is it worth risking student disfavor by giving cumulative exams? If those exams promote long-term retention (and this isn't the only research work supporting that finding), the risk is worth taking. Students can be told about this research, content covered previously can be regularly mentioned in light of current content, and teachers (or high-scoring classmates) can work with students on those study strategies that effectively prepare them for cumulative questions.

Reference: Lawrence, N.K. (2013). Cumulative exams in the introductory psychology course. *Teaching Psychology,* 40 (1), 15–19.

Reprinted from *The Teaching Professor,* 27.2 (2013): 6.

An Electronic Leap: Web-based Quizzes

By Jan D. Andersen, California State University, Sacramento, California

Like Mark Twain's famous jumping frog of Calaveras County, many teachers are weighed down with the thoughts, traditions, and technologies of the past, unable to make that giant electronic leap, even though their colleges and universities have invested much to provide the necessary technology.

Four years ago, I leaped and changed my approach to quizzing. I eliminated all in-class quizzes. I stopped using quizzes as summative assessments and starting using them to provide students a management tool for keeping up with the assigned readings.

Now all of my quizzes are electronically administered outside the classroom through a commercial, web-based management system. (Although there are several software systems available today, I use WebCT because our university has already purchased it for instructors' use.) For those who may want to make this same leap, I would like to offer some points to consider when designing and administering web-based quizzes:

1. **Single attempt or multiple attempts.** Although web-based quizzes can be designed to let students take a quiz any number of times, I generally allow my students three attempts at any one quiz. I let my students know the first day of class that even though points earned on quizzes count toward their final course grade, the primary purpose of the weekly quizzes is to help them keep up with the reading and "not to ruin their GPA."

If they do not do well on the first quiz attempt, they can go back and more carefully examine the reading material. As long as the instructor uses non-essay questions (i.e., multiple-choice, true-false, matching, short-answer), all quiz attempts are graded electronically, thus reducing the instructor's overall grading burden.

2. **Same or different version.** Because of security concerns that I'll discuss in a minute, many of my colleagues set up their web-based quizzes so that on any attempt each student gets a customized quiz. By the teacher providing many more questions than needed, the management software will randomly pick for each student the desired number of questions.

This approach accomplishes summative objectives, but that's not my purpose. Besides, writing and uploading the questions is the most time-consuming aspect of using web-based quizzes.

3. **Level of difficulty.** Because I allow multiple attempts on any one quiz, I often ask questions that are more difficult than I would have asked with a single-attempt design. Contrary to some student views, this doesn't mean that I deliberately try to "trick" students, but I try to ask questions that require a more in-depth understanding of the reading material.

Further, if several attempts are allowed, multiple-choice questions need to be written with a sufficient number of response choices so that success depends on something more than repeated guesses. Increasing the difficulty level prompts discussion in class and gives me valuable feedback. Students may take the quiz during a one-week interval (more details in the next point), and this leaves time to ask quiz-related questions in class.

4. **Duration.** Web-based quizzes can be designed to allow students any amount of time to complete a quiz. Additionally, students can be allowed a specific time frame in which to complete a quiz. Because I want the students to keep up with the assigned reading, I allow a week for them to take the corresponding quiz. And I limit the duration of any attempt to no more than 15 minutes for a 10-question, multiple-choice quiz (i.e., 1.5 minutes per question).

I've had no students complain that they are not able to finish the quizzes in the allotted time. In addition, by giving students a full week to complete a quiz, I have virtually eliminated the problems associated with student absences and makeup quizzes.

5. Security. Although web-based quizzes generally are administered on password-protected systems, one of the disadvantages of giving unsupervised quizzes online is that the instructor never knows for sure who is actually taking the quiz. Students can give their login information to others, or groups of students can congregate to take quizzes together.

Additionally, students quickly discover that the quiz questions are not secure and can easily be copied, printed, or emailed. Consequently, I inform them before the first quiz is due that they can print the questions after their first attempt and use them to locate the correct responses in the reading material. However, because of the lack of security, I do not use the Web for major exams.

After four years of trial and error with web-based quizzes, I have no desire to leap backward. Electronic technology has not only eliminated the need for in-class quizzes but also eliminated my weekly chore of grading quizzes. It has freed up more classroom time, reduced my use of departmental resources, and given me many more quiz options.

And, most important, my leap has resulted in an approach that makes my students more successful learners.

Reprinted from *The Teaching Professor,* 18.3 (2004): 4.

Quizzes Boost Comprehension and Confidence

By Scott Warnock, Penn State Berks, Pennsylvania

Years ago, to encourage my students to read, I began opening class with short, user-friendly reading quizzes. I soon realized these quizzes accomplished a variety of objectives, and quizzing evolved into an important learning component of my courses. If you share some of the objectives described below and are seeking a way to jump-start the beginning of your classes, you might find this quizzing strategy useful.

Classroom management: When I assign reading, I begin the next class with a quiz. I don't allow makeups, so students who are late or miss class also miss the quiz. That gets students to class on time. I ask between four and 10 straightforward, short-answer (and I do mean short) questions that I read out loud. I keep the questions simple so the quizzes are easy to grade; I grade 40 quizzes in about 15 minutes.

Quizzes count for between 15 percent and 20 percent of the course grade. I soften my seemingly tough makeup policy by allowing students to drop 10 percent to 20 percent of their quizzes (four out of 19 in a recent course). My goal is not to punish, and I think students who completed 15 quizzes still did a lot of good work.

Comprehension: Not only do these quizzes help students read, they also encourage them to read closely and actually to reread. Recently a student complained about the quizzes, but I pointed out that on my way to class I saw him and fellow classmates reviewing the readings in the hall. "What are the chances you would reread your material before class if it weren't for the quiz?" I asked. His wry smile told me that he understood.

I ask quiz questions about the order of plot elements, macro events, brief summaries of key points, and what happens to major characters. I don't ask about plot nuances, specific dates, or ambiguous points. Sometimes I ask vocabulary questions, reading the sentence with the vocabulary word directly from the text. My goal with comprehension is for students to have a clear understanding of the reading overall, and the quizzes help them read with more attention.

Confidence: I opt for easy questions because if the quizzes are too hard, students will be stressed, and that undermines my objectives. If I feel the students need more challenge, I use extra credits to pose tough questions. I even try to make the quizzes fun because I want students to feel positive as they begin class.

After I collect the quizzes, I ask each question out loud, relying on a community spirit to answer the questions and resolve discrepancies. If students call out answers that are close or reveal the question was unclear, I always move toward leniency—and I do this in front of the students. This further reinforces that I'm not using quizzes to burn them.

Going over the quiz right after they've completed it gives the students immediate feedback. They don't wonder if they missed a question. Most of the time, students who did their reading realize they just achieved a 100. By not using terribly difficult quizzes and tending toward leniency, I often end up with a class brimming with confidence, making for an easy segue to discussion.

Conversation: The open quiz review atmosphere builds conversation in several ways. Most students have already spoken, so they are loose and ready to talk. The quiz review also encourages exchanges between students. Students might ask other students how they got a particular answer.

Sometimes they share "high fives" or congratulations. Students often defend incorrect answers with textual evidence, or differing views of a key point prompt side discussions that I can easily introduce to the whole group. I sometimes design quiz questions as an outline for the class discussion that day.

The quiz reviews help develop and define the culture of that particular class. Admittedly, reviews can be boisterous, but I usually find this energy constructive and easy to channel into deeper issues. And my students respond positively to the quizzes. One recently wrote on my course evaluation form that the quizzes "created a little man in the back of my mind that told me to read." Quizzes not only encourage my students to read closely, but they also create an energy that strengthens my rapport with them and helps build an open learning environment in my classroom.

Reprinted from *The Teaching Professor,* 18.3 (2004): 5.

Testing Learning, Not Anxiety

By Francine S. Glazer, Kean University, New Jersey

In any course, students can easily become demoralized if their first exam grade is lower than expected. When the morale of a class decreases, so does the level of participation, enthusiasm, and interest in the subject. If anxiety is too high, less learning occurs. In my efforts to test students' knowledge without provoking undue anxiety, I have developed a number of approaches and borrowed some from colleagues. I'd like to share a sample.

Exam design and student preparation

- Prepare students in advance of the exam so they know what to expect with regard to topics, format, and testing style. A well-designed, single-sheet handout, accompanied by a few minutes of discussion in class, works well. Making old exams available also gives students clear ideas about what to expect.
- If you give essay exams, consider giving students the questions (or at least the topics) in advance. Giving questions usually results in answers that are more synthesized and detailed.
- Use a variety of question types. Even better, offer students a choice of exam formats; for example, an objective exam with an optional essay. Students could then elect to take an exam that is 75 percent objective questions and 25 percent essay, or they could choose to take the same exam without the essay component. Both exams may be worth the same point totals. If the student opts not to do the essay, the objective questions are each worth proportionately more points.

Course design

- Give one test early in the semester. Call it a practice test, or make it worth less than the other exams. This gives students a lower-stakes vehicle for assessing their performance at a point in the course when they can still correct the amount and way they are studying.

- Base the grade on more than a midterm and a final. More lower-stakes assignments reduce anxiety.
- Consider dropping one exam score or counting them all and the final but with this provision: give a cumulative final, and *replace* the lowest hourly exam grade with a duplicate of the final. For example, if a student earned a 90, 78, and 87 on the hourly exams and an 85 on the final, I would replace the 78 with a duplicate of the final, 85. Grade calculations are then based on the three exams (now 90, 85, and 87) and the final exam grade of 85.

Reward/incentive mechanisms

   • Encourage students to continue learning material after the exam by offering them an optional retest of the hourly exam. Use the same content, but vary the format using different question types on the retest. You can require students to accept the retest grade, regardless of whether it is better or worse, or you can let them keep whichever score is higher. The second approach motivates more retests, and if students are retesting, they are continuing to review the material.

- Reward improvement. If a student's second exam is better than the first one, add one-third of the difference back to the first score. So if the first exam was a 70 and the second a 79, the first score gets three points added to it.
- Reward outstanding performance. If a student has 90 percent or better on all the hourly exams, consider exempting those students from the comprehensive final. They have already demonstrated considerable mastery of the material.

   These approaches can be used in a variety of disciplines, and one or several of them may be just what it takes to keep your students learning with enthusiasm.

Reprinted from *The Teaching Professor,* 14.6 (2000): 7.

Rethinking Assessment

By Jerry Reed, Valencia Community College, Orlando, Florida, and Nancy Small Reed

In large, introductory courses, student learning is typically assessed with machine-scored multiple-choice tests. This approach works well when the course is a new one or the instructor teaches part time. Other busy faculty members are persuaded to adopt the approach by the helpful test item bank that comes with the text.

But students still see these tests as overly abstract, anxiety-provoking, and contrived. Based on our experience, we think that there are better ways to assess learning.

An approach that has worked well for both of us, in courses as diverse as introductory computer programming, organizational behavior, interpersonal skills, and industrial/organizational psychology, is that of using project-based exams. In this case, student learning is defined primarily by improved performance on realistic tasks relevant to course content.

Programming students should be able to use course content such as algorithms, languages, and tools in further programming courses and actual work tasks. This means being able to understand the typical work demands for entry-level programmers as well as being better able to coordinate efforts with other programmers and project members.

Business students need to function as leaders or effective team members on group tasks in class and at work. Although we cannot measure performance after the class directly, we can use project-based tests to assess student performance on model tasks in the classroom.

Typical work tasks faced by many professional services employees, including programmers, project managers, team leaders, and supervisors, include addressing abstract problems under time pressure. The more guided practice students have dealing with these types of problems, the more likely they are to perform satisfactorily on the job.

Considerable research has shown that merely attending class, or even memorizing the text and lecture materials, is not enough to guarantee improved performance. Project assignments make course content more realistic and less difficult for students to remember and apply.

Multiple-choice questions may lack detail and context and appear to need a "magic insight" for solution. When that insight is not immediately forthcoming during the exam, anxiety sets in and further hinders the expression of learned material. This is just as destructive to performance in a business, management, or programming setting as "math anxiety" can be in solving algebra problems. Project-based approaches largely avoid this situation.

By midterm, all of our homework and class activities are project based, whether a full-blown programming project or several smaller business problem scenarios. Since instructor enthusiasm consistently shows a strong relationship to student satisfaction with a course, we pick projects and scenarios of interest to us. To enhance realism, we present the content as customer requirements, staff reports, consultant advice, or company procedures.

This takes the form of text, web-based materials, and examples from the workplace in addition to required readings. Students are assigned content to share with the class, either via the class website or directly in class. Working in teams, the class produces a program or solves workplace problems that are more complex than all but the very ablest students could do on their own. We help students accomplish the project successfully by ensuring that particularly promising students are seeded into each group.

The goal is to make students comfortable using course content to produce products prior to the final examination. Then we derive final exam questions structured around these class-produced projects. These questions can often be objectively scored and are viewed as quite fair by students. After all, they helped develop the projects. There can be multiple correct answers for some questions, as in life.

Here are some sample test items using class projects as vehicles for evaluating, and perhaps enhancing, student learning:

Recognizing concepts: (1) Which line(s) show a Boolean operator being used? (2) What management error does this statement reflect? "Josh Smith didn't work hard enough to accurately complete his report on employee absenteeism, while I couldn't finish my report on diversity training due to inadequate information from the overseas division."

What-If questions: What line numbers in the program will be executed if X equals 5 at line 300?

Why questions: (1) Why was the program loop from lines 413 to 418 introduced into our program? (2) Why was intrinsic commitment important to the management team in the Amalgamated scenario?

Next action/best action questions: (1) Based on the information provided above concerning Maria's problem with her team, what is the best action Maria could take next? (Responses generated using class discussions and other course material). (2) How could the function on lines 352 to 376 be rewritten to use real-valued variables?

For those wanting to assess a student's choice of action in more depth or to assess the quality of the student's reasoning more fully, multiple-choice questions can be followed up with an "Explain your response" short answer or longer essay response.

These are particularly useful with items that have more than one acceptable course of action, as do many project-based questions. The student's explanation can elevate a marginally correct response to a "best" response and should be scored accordingly.

Finally, as the focus is on applied learning, it makes sense to have the exam be "open book," "open notes," "open Web," or all three with few negative consequences. Yes, some students might happen upon an example in the text very similar to a traditional exam problem or might even be able to cut and paste a snippet of relevant code from the Web.

However, they will be able to find only the most general sorts of advantage from the text and Web when test questions focus on their unique project(s). As our real purpose is for them to improve future performance, learning late is better than not learning at all.

Reprinted from *The Teaching Professor,* 21.8 (2007): 1.

New Kind of "Space" for Quizzes

By Audrey L. Deterding, Indiana University Southeast, Indiana

Quizzes are standard in many college classrooms, and determining how to best use this learning format generates a variety of discussion and suggestions—if you regularly read The Teaching Professor you've seen any number published here. I too continue to search for ways to inspire the often dull quiz routine.

In an effort to bring new strategies to the classroom and keep student engagement high, I have recently discovered a successful strategy that encourages a sense of community in class, offers students an opportunity to engage in collaborative learning, and motivates students to come to class prepared. Let me explain how it works.

First, the chalkboard or whiteboard in the classroom becomes what I call a "community space." Two students are selected to use the space. They have three minutes at the beginning of class, before the quiz, to write anything from the materials assigned for that day on the board. I use a random process to select the students who write on the board. I allow students to decline the offer to participate, but I do not select alternates if one or both students decide not to write on that day.

Whatever information is put up on the board can be used by the rest of the class on the quiz. The students who write on the board are allowed to talk with one another; often, they begin by quickly planning what they will place on the board and who will cover what information. The other students in the class may not talk or consult their notes or the book during the three minutes when their classmates are placing information in the community space.

As the course progresses, students start being able to anticipate the kind of information I will be asking for on the quiz, and that's what they write in the community space. Most pairs tend to use the last 15 to 30 seconds of time to check each other's work and to add missing information.

When I first introduced this idea to the class, there were some reservations, especially about my being "fair" when selecting the students. Here's what we decided I would do: I call on one student and ask that student to designate a number. Then I call on a second student and that student tells me "up" or "down."

Based on those responses, I go to my class roster and start with the name of the person who gave me the number and then I count up or down by that number. That's the first student selected. From that student's name I continuing to count up (or down) using the same number, and that's the second student.

Although students have the opportunity to decline to write, I have yet to have a student do so. Sometimes the information they provide is limited, but very rarely is it inaccurate. I've found the expectation that they may have to share information in the community space motivates most students to closely read the assigned materials. They want to help their classmates perform well on the quizzes, and they don't want to appear lazy or irresponsible to their peers.

The three minutes allocated limits the amount of help fellow classmates receive. Consequently, students who do not prepare for class will not perform well on the quiz, even though they have access to this information. I've observed that this approach encourages collaborative learning and creates a sense of community among the students. It also gets students coming to class prepared, and I think it makes the quizzes a more positive and useful learning experience.

Reprinted from *The Teaching Professor,* 24.9 (2010): 6.

Chapter 2:
Grading Papers

Too Many Papers: Two Solutions

By John Sturtridge, Cambrian College, Ontario, Canada

I mostly teach basic technical writing, and I face the same problem that confronts many of us who teach writing. It's hard enough getting students to do the assignments and almost impossible to get them to do a first draft. But writing takes practice, and if you require students to practice, that leads to an inevitable mountain of papers to grade.

At my college, the trend is toward bigger classes and fewer course hours in English. This makes giving students the chance to practice all the more important and providing the necessary feedback all the more challenging. I'd like to share a couple of solutions I've devised that help me deal with both these problems.

I try to have students do at least one draft before they hand in a graded assignment. Some of my students refuse. They don't do anything if it does not generate a grade. Arguing that submitting a draft and getting feedback will likely yield a higher grade doesn't work. The joy of doing nothing trumps the possibility of a better grade.

Even accounting for refusniks, this approach often leaves me offering feedback on two pieces of writing for every graded assignment, and that's a lot of work. Here's my solution. I tell students that if their draft is an A-level piece of work, I will put that grade on their draft and give them a choice: they may keep that grade or do the formal assignment in the hopes of earning an even higher grade.

(At my college grades are numerical, with anything 80 and over considered an A grade. Students with an 84 might feel they could do even better. A student with an A- might be willing to work for an A.) All the other drafts are returned with feedback but no grades. Those who do not submit A-level work must do the graded assignment.

With the bar set high—A-level or do more work on that paper—I see students putting a lot more effort into their draft papers. This isn't true of all students, but of more than I expected. I almost always get some A-level work. If a student shows me that he or she can write an A-level incident report on the first go (after my brilliant lectures, of course), then I don't need to see the student do it twice to believe it. This reduces the amount of work the student must produce and the amount of grading I must do.

Additionally, or as a stand-alone alternative, I sometimes allow teams of two to do the writing assignment. This is my second solution for reducing the time I must spend providing feedback and grades. The team approach yields some quality drafts even if offered without the A-level carrot.

Two students working (or arguing) with each other over how to do an assignment seems to produce a good number of well-done pieces of work. I restrict this to teams of two. In larger groups the work is not always divided evenly among members.

I have tried other, blunter approaches to force students to do drafts. For example, I tried setting up a rule that no graded assignment could be submitted if a draft had not been submitted first. The approach was not successful. Students didn't devote much effort to the drafts—they handed in any piece of crap (the technical term) just to meet the requirement.

This actually increased the amount of time I spent grading. Commenting on poor writing is more time-consuming than commenting on well-done work. Besides, it's a punitive approach, which the students recognize and resent.

One of my courses this semester has more than 100 students (broken into four sections for students from two different disciplines). Two reports plus a number of other writing assignments are required in the course. The two reports mean 400 papers to grade if each student does a draft and a revised final report.

Add the other assignments, not to mention work in other courses I deliver, and I have more grading than I can handle. Offering the A-level carrot yields a more realistic amount of grading, especially combined with the team approach.

Although I speak to this from an English teacher's perspective, I have no doubt the approach would work for pretty much any discipline. If you are facing similar grading loads, and I am certain I am not alone, then you might give these approaches a try.

Reprinted from *The Teaching Professor,* 26.6 (2012): 8.

Incorporating Process Pedagogy into Grading Student Essays

By Matt Birkenhauer, Northern Kentucky University, Kentucky

As a very young teacher, I remember pulling all-nighters (not all that infrequently) to get my students' essays back within the one-week limit I set for myself. Even in those days this "cram grading" was miserable and exhausting; but now at 50—especially with the added responsibilities of husband, father, and homeowner—it's all but impossible.

However, it's a prospect I rarely face nowadays, mostly because over the years I've developed a system where I grade student papers the same way I encourage students to write—that is, I've incorporated a process approach to grading student essays. I'd like to share it with others interested in providing students thoughtful and timely feedback on written work.

The process starts with something I call "dipping." I "dip" by going through a batch of student essays to make sure everything is in order. For example, for all submitted essays I require a grading rubric, a rough draft, and a final draft. (For papers using sources, I also require a works cited page.) So—while watching TV at night or sitting in my home office as my kids play elsewhere—I'll dip.

In addition to making sure that everything is in order, dipping also allows me to skim the first page or so of the essay. An experienced professor can often discern a great deal about the whole essay during this quick review of the opening paragraphs. For example, this part of the process gives me a feel for which are the strong and the weak essays in the batch.

The next step in my process involves the use of sticky notes, usually of the 4-by-6-inch size (though any size you're comfortable with will work). At this stage I read through the entire essay and then comment on its strengths and weaknesses.

On one sticky note, for a personal experience essay, I wrote "Though Ashley sometimes uses more words than she needs to, she tells a pretty good story, with suspense and buildup. The weakest part for me was the conclusion. What could she do to improve this?" Obviously, I'm not completely certain of my full response here, but that's OK; I don't have to be at this point. That's a benefit of approaching grading as a process.

The advantage of sticky notes is that their very size encourages me to be concise. In addition to my sticky note comments, I also "mark" papers in this stage of the process, in the sense of pointing out sentence boundary and other problems; but I don't heavily edit the essays, since the research from the last 30 years makes clear that bleeding all over a student's essay isn't all that useful.

In the last stage of this process, which is the *only* stage if you're reduced to cram grading, I comment directly on the student's grading rubric; that is, I transform my sticky note "writer-based" comments (to borrow from Linda Flower in an article in *College English*) into the reader-based comments the student sees.

Because I use grading rubrics, I needn't reprise everything that is wrong with a particular essay and can distill from my sticky note comments what is most germane to a student's revising his or her essay. With the high A essays, I generally just give a verbal pat on the back. With essays in the B range and below, I comment more, though usually no more than a brief paragraph. My comments also include underlined or asterisked parts of the grading rubric, sometimes with brief comments in the margin.

Although this process approach may seem more work, it's really not. By the time I'm reading an essay for the third time, I'm more often than not skimming rather than reading the essay in its entirety. And my process approach to grading, like the process approach to writing itself, is often recursive—frequently dipping, for example, blends with marking and even commenting directly on a rubric, if I feel so disposed and have already read the essay in conference or commented on it as a rough draft.

Finally, I think a process approach to grading is fairer to the student. If you have only one shot to respond—that is, if you try to grade a batch of papers in essentially a single sitting—are you giving a truly reflective response? This is particularly a problem for those essays that when first read make us scratch our heads. But if you give yourself two or three times to ruminate over such an essay, your response is likely to be more helpful because you're being more thoughtful.

Reprinted from *The Teaching Professor,* 22.5 (2008): 4.

Death by Paper: Ten Secrets for Survival

By Frances S. Johnson, Rowan University, New Jersey

Numerous researchers have identified the correlation between writing and thinking. Others have explored the complexities involved in the writing process. Despite the volumes of research that document the multiple benefits that accrue from writing, many faculty members are reluctant to assign much, because if assigned it must be graded.

Getting out from under the piles of research papers, reflective essays, reaction papers, and journals can be daunting. Electronic media expedites student writing, but what appears in blogs, wikis, and Web discussions needs a response. In the past 20 years as a writing teacher, I have found several techniques that can help faculty in any discipline use writing to achieve its many benefits and still manage the paper load.

1. Grade with a timer.

Set it for 10 to 15 minutes. When the bell goes off, write final comments and then move on. This activity can help train you to be more mindful of your time and keep you focused. In most instances, after spending 15 minutes with an essay, you already have a grade in mind.

2. Read the whole paper, but correct and line edit only a few paragraphs. Leave the rest unmarked—read, but unmarked. Add a final comment.

Correcting every grammar, content, and punctuation error is you doing the student's work for him or her. Correct a short section of the paper. Ask the student to do the rest and come to your office with the revisions.

3. Use minimal marking.

Minimal marking is a system for grading that puts a great deal of the responsibility for corrections and revisions on the student. Instead of putting in commas, fixing sentence errors, or addressing other mechanical problems, put a check on the line to indicate that a problem exists there. Save your comments for matters of substance.

4. Make and use a rubric.

Providing a rubric for the writing assignment benefits you and your students. Creating it forces you to think of the major and minor elements of the assignment and to clarify any hidden expectations you have. You can assign points to criteria; use a scale of poor to excellent; or just use check minus, check, and check plus.

In addition to saving time, a rubric makes your grading more effective and focused. Rubrics also benefit students; knowing what's expected helps them prepare the assignment.

5. Write a letter or memo to the class about the strengths and weaknesses of the papers.

Often many students experience the same problem with an assignment. In report writing, the formats may be incorrect. Documentation may be a problem. On the other hand, maybe everyone wrote a particularly good thesis statement. Effective feedback addresses both strengths and weaknesses. Take all those comments you would normally write 20 or so times and put them in a letter addressed to the whole class.

6. Make positive comments on one side of the paper and negative comments on the other.

Ample research documents that instructors make many more negative comments than positive ones. Not only that, but the negative comments are much longer, while positive comments are brief ("good job"). If you write negative comments on one side of the paper and positive comments on the other, you will become conscious of how your comments are proportioned and make adjustments.

7. Scan the papers and sort into three stacks: very good, average, poor.

A quick read can tell you a great deal. This fast review of writing with no marking is called holistic reading. It helps you make an early evaluation of the paper's overall quality.

8. Select one to three major problems to comment on.

Many teachers think they need to point out every flaw and problem with an assignment. This is not only unnecessary, but it also frustrates students. They become confused and don't know what to fix first. Comment on the major issues in a paper or report. Give clear instructions for revision. Leave the rest alone.

9. Reduce your comment wording.

Try learning to write shorter phrases such as "Needs development," "Needs a clear focus," "'Needs a 'so what?'" or "Lacks required sources." This strategy has the added bonus of adding a level of consistency to your grading.

10. "See me briefly."

Many times it is more efficient to explain something verbally than it is to write it down. It may take me a long time to explain that I assigned an argument and received a report or that the experiments in the lab report were incorrectly performed. Telling the student that not only saves you time, but also it allows the student to ask you questions. Students grasp the problem better after even a short conversation.

Reprinted from *The Teaching Professor,* 20.6 (2000): 1.

Global Perspective on Responding to Student Writing

By Kathy Gehr, College of Charleston, South Carolina

Faculty who assign writing in their courses know that it enhances student learning, yet many do not require written assignments because they have learned that evaluating student work takes a lot of time. Even the most seasoned writing teachers often spend five minutes per page responding to student texts. With 20 students in a class and a three-page paper, that comes to five intense hours of grading per assignment. For teachers who have less experience responding to student writing, grading consumes even more time.

Too often conversations about efficient grading focus exclusively on the process of marking final drafts. Approaches such as minimal marking or grading sheets can reduce the amount of time involved in marking those drafts; however, they are not always effective.

To make student writing a rich and enriching component of a course, it must be embedded in the course's design and classroom activities. We must think of designing assignments, working with drafts, and grading final drafts as an interconnected process. The following strategies make grading shortcuts on final drafts more likely to work for everyone:

Designing assignments

- *Sequence written assignments from less to more complex intellectual work.*
  Think of your assignments as guides to the kinds of thinking and writing that your discipline requires. If, for example, you want students in a psychology class to write a literature review of five recent studies on the effects of antidepressants on children, start with a short assignment that asks students to write a one-paragraph summary of one study and a one-paragraph analysis of that same study. When the student is asked to synthesize five studies, she will know how to begin. In fact, she already will have started.

- *Discuss sample responses to major written assignments.* Sample papers should offer a clear fit with the assignment at hand but should not be so successful that they intimidate students. Usually a solid B paper makes an effective sample draft.

As for the content of sample papers, topics based on previous course material or on engaging examples from popular culture are much more effective than a direct hit on the assignment's topic.

- *Use grading criteria or rubrics to set a tone of encouragement rather than of punishment.* Define the terms that you use in these rubrics. If you ask for a "reasonably complex" thesis statement, provide an example of what one looks like. If you require secondary sources, list a few sources so that your students can distinguish them from primary sources. Format with hollow boxes instead of bullets, ask questions rather than give commands, emphasize what an effective paper does rather than what a lousy paper does not do, and arrange criteria from most to least important.

Working with drafts

- *Personalize your responses to student work.* Instead of automatically responding to every student's work, a process that often reinforces a tell-me-what-you-want mentality, require that students ask you two questions about their drafts. The more time and effort that they put into their questions, the more useful your feedback is likely to be.

This sends the message that you respect the student's ownership of her ideas and want to provide feedback that makes her draft a better paper rather than a closer version of some perfect paper that exists in your own mind.

- *Emphasize your role as a reader rather than as an evaluator.* Rather than saying, "This essay lacks effective transitions," say, "Sally, I was interested in the point that you make about Hamlet's insanity in paragraph two, but as a reader, I was confused about how this point is related to the quote from Claudius that you discuss in paragraph three. How does Claudius's language affect our reaction to Hamlet's behavior? This is the question that you need to answer at the beginning of paragraph three."

This example offers a question that guides the student to the next step in the revision process.

- *Make writing a communal problem that everyone in the class is working together to solve.* Encourage students to present revisions of paragraphs or sentences to the class as a whole. Schedule group writing conferences. Mention during class time the conversations that you have had with students outside class: "That's a good question, Mark. This is the same problem that John was struggling with in his essay. He decided to integrate a different kind of source to define his terms. Would you mind telling us about that, John? How did you decide which definition would work best?"

- *Use familiar examples and storytelling to create a shorthand way of talking about common writing issues.* In class I might say, "Good conclusions are more like buffets than plated dinners. An effective conclusion offers a clear focus—Chinese, Indian, or Italian—but doesn't force you to eat your moo shu in a pancake."

Later, when a student offers a conclusion with no clear controlling idea, I might say, "I feel like I'm being served beer at a breakfast buffet. You offer a lot of good ideas, but I don't understand the logic of how they are related to one another." Examples like this not only take the edge off the criticism, they also help students understand shorthand comments on final drafts—"Conclusion lacks focus and is too repetitive."

Reprinted from *The Teaching Professor,* 19.1 (2005): 1.

The Writing Process

By Paul T. Corrigan, Southeastern University, Florida

Though tons of attention has been paid to what good college writing looks like and to how bad student writing typically is, the "writing process movement" has made a radical breakthrough in terms of getting more students to actually write better.

Simply put, the idea behind the writing process movement is this: we ought to pay attention not just to *what* students write but also to *how* they go about writing. In practical terms, this means that when we assign writing, we would do well not just to give instructions on what the final product should look like but also to give instructions on the process students should take to get to such a final product and (this is key!) do something to hold students accountable for engaging in that process.

On a personal note, I should say that I consider the idea of the writing process—and, more significantly, the practice of the writing process—to be the single most important thing that I learned when I was a student. The skill of engaging in the writing process allowed me to learn deeply throughout college, gave me a significant advantage in graduate school, and set me on track to be a productive scholarly writer.

Now I realize that the reason the writing process made such a difference for me is because I "caught it" and engaged myself in it. I realize that what happened to me is not likely to happen for many of my students. Nonetheless, I still maintain that most students can benefit from being instructed on and held accountable for the writing process.

Though students are often taught about the writing process in their first-year writing courses, what they learn there needs to be developed and reinforced in every other course they take that requires them to write.

On a practical note, paying attention to the writing process as a teacher means giving instruction on and holding students accountable for such things as invention, drafting, feedback, revision, and editing. The more important the assignment, the more attention the process should receive.

I like to think in terms of worst practices, best practices, and good enough practices. The idea is to avoid the worst practices because they are counterproductive; understand what the best practices are so as to have something to measure whatever practices one ends up using against (and in case one ever has the resources to implement them); and settle for the good enough practices because that's the best that can reasonably be done in many circumstances.

In terms of the writing process, worst, best, and good enough practices include such things as the following.

Worst practices

Give instructions for a writing assignment, collect it when it's due, and then grade and correct the work. If this is the way that professors assign writing, then we may know why so many are not only frustrated with the quality of the writing they receive from students but also overwhelmed by the amount of work it takes to grade papers.

This assign-collect-correct approach should be avoided as much as possible for any substantial writing assignments, though assigning and collecting (but not "correcting") are perfectly okay for informal, low-stakes writing assignments, such as journal writing, where the actual quality of the writing does not matter so much.

Best practices

Give written instructions; give and have students analyze examples; have students come up with evaluation criteria; conduct and require brainstorming sessions; conduct and require drafting sessions; break the assignment into smaller parts; collect drafts of different parts of the assignment; assign informal peer review; assign formal peer review; give instructor feedback on a draft; conduct and require revision and rewriting sessions; conduct and require editing sessions; and collect and grade with a rubric, comparing the revisions made against the feedback already given.

Obviously, teaching and facilitating the writing process through all these best practices is time-intensive. But it does yield results. The full-scale implementation and support of the writing process is usually reserved for classes that focus on writing (e.g., English composition, writing in the discipline courses, thesis hours, capstone courses, etc.) and classes that focus on some other content but are nonetheless writing-intensive.

Good enough practices

Give written instructions, assign brainstorming, give and have students analyze examples, assign drafting, assign informal peer review, assign revision, collect and grade with a checklist.

Such practices often take less effort than the worst practices and produce better results. They do, of course, cost something in terms of class time and calendar space. But adding a few supports for the writing process generally pays off in terms of the quality of writing and learning that results.

Taking the process slowly may mean that less "gets covered," but it also means that what does get covered gets learned more deeply.

Reprinted from *The Teaching Professor,* 27.2 (2013): 4.

No Time for Revision?

By Kevin Brown, Lee University, Tennessee

The 2008 Faculty Survey of Student Engagement found that "about 47% of faculty members teaching lower division courses and 54% of those teaching upper-division courses thought it was important or very important for their students to write more than one draft of a paper."

It is troubling to note that less than half of the professors who teach first-year students believe that those students should revise their papers and that only slightly more than half of those teaching upper-division courses think similarly. Nonetheless, a significant number of professors think students should do more revision across their educational careers.

The 2008 National Survey of Student Engagement reports that 75 percent of first-year students received instructor feedback on paper drafts, but only 63 percent of seniors did. Similarly, 74 percent of first-year students stated that they received feedback from a peer, friend, or family member, while only 64 percent of seniors did. When it comes to visiting a campus writing center, the numbers are even more problematic: 31 percent of first-year students made such a visit, but only 19 percent of seniors did.

If professors believe that preparing multiple drafts helps students write better papers and think more deeply about a subject, then why don't they have students doing more revision work?

The answer is obvious: it takes too much time. First, professor time, for reading and providing feedback, and second, class time that should be used for covering the content. I'd like to suggest several ways students can do multiple drafts that address both of these time issues.

Peers can help with feedback on early drafts. In my upper-division courses, I have students turn in a rough draft to me but also to a group of students that I select to be their peer editing group. I have a sheet that guides those peer groups through the process. It mirrors the issues I look for when grading a final draft. The drafts are read over the weekend, and then feedback is delivered during one 50-minute class period. It might be possible for this feedback exchange to happen outside class or online.

From some of my colleagues, I learned an abbreviated approach to conferencing with upper-division students. I read the entire rough draft but focus on only one or two pages, which limits my time investment but still enables me to deal with major concerns such as thesis or evidence.

When I conferenced with first-year students this semester, I told them that I would read their first and last paragraphs and one body paragraph of their choosing. This approach enabled me to look at how they used evidence in their papers, as well as their theses and conclusions. It also shortened conferences from 10 minutes to five minutes, which, given my 60 composition students, saved five hours.

Using peer editing groups and reading rough drafts outside class do not affect content coverage in the course. Many professors believe that they will need to give up days of class if they are going to integrate any aspect of writing into their courses. Although I would argue that spending class time teaching writing is valuable and not a waste of time, there are still ways to integrate writing with course content. Let me share a couple of examples.

In an American novel course I teach, I have the students read criticism on the novel we're discussing and write short response papers. I offer feedback on those papers, which students can then use not only to improve their general writing skills but also as a foundation for their longer papers. When students write about course content, they must dig more deeply into the reading at the same time they are developing their writing skills.

Almost every college or university has a writing center on campus. We often encourage our first-year students to visit it, but we then think upper-division students shouldn't need to. Since most writing centers are staffed by upper-division students who perform well in writing courses, graduate students, or even composition faculty, upper-division students can still benefit from visiting such centers. Any opportunity to get feedback from someone who writes well is a chance for valuable input. I think we ought to encourage, if not require, our upper-division students to spend time with a tutor at the writing center.

Having students write multiple drafts does not need to take up more instructor time or take away from course content. Instead, it can add to both. Revision improves the quality of student papers, which saves professors time grading and means students spend more time thinking about the content they have probably come to understand more fully. Perhaps professors need to revise their ideas about how they teach writing.

Reprinted from *The Teaching Professor*, 23.3 (2009): 5.

Writing Comments
That Lead to Learning

By Susan M. Taylor, Andrew University, Michigan

Instructors who require papers spend a good deal of time emphasizing the importance of audience and purpose in writing. Writers who remember their readers and their writing objectives are much more likely to use good judgment about the decisions that go into creating an effective piece of writing. This is equally true of the comments instructors write on students' papers. I'd like to share some suggestions, some of which I learned the hard way.

Students often react first to the number of comments on the paper. They look to see how much the instructor "bled" on their papers. They may not even read overall comments that appear at the end. Sometimes it helps to put those comments up front so that students see them first.

Notes in the margins of the papers tend to be sketchy. With little room in the margins, instructors use more underlining, coding, and abbreviating. Many marginal notes simply label a problem without further explanation or example.

For instance, I have written "There are stronger works for your POV" on papers, not thinking that POV (for point of view) may be an unfamiliar acronym. Not only does this feedback puzzle and frustrate students, but it doesn't help them improve.

There is a difference between an explanation that simply shows the students how to reword or rewrite something and an in-depth explanation that discusses the reasoning behind the suggested change. For example, in a legal brief for my Business Law class, a student wrote, "This is an appeal from the judgment of the St. Joseph County Superior Court, by a jury, that the defendant was guilty of check forgery."

After having spent so much time on the papers that my hand ached, I gave in to writer's cramp and simply underlined "the judgment" and "by the jury." Fortunately, the student came to me and asked what I meant.

On one of my first papers (when my hand was fresh and cramp-free), I wrote, "Watch your language. A jury convicts or acquits but cannot render a judgment. The court enters a judgment on the jury's verdict." This comment is a more useful explanation.

Instructors must balance the positive and negative comments, remembering the importance of positive feedback. It motivates students, is essential to improvement, and builds confidence. If students are told why something is good, they can do more of it subsequently. Papers lacking any positive feedback tend to lead to poor student morale.

Closely related is the overall tone of the comments. Instructors need to keep the tone professional. Constructive criticism goes a long way, but destructive criticism goes an even longer way. Once someone destroys your self-confidence as a writer, it is almost impossible to write well.

How many is too many? Instructors should monitor the number of comments they write on students' papers. Although it may be tempting to comment on everything, the workload quickly becomes intolerable, and too much feedback may overwhelm the students. They find it difficult to prioritize the comments and tend to retreat into simple and safe writing in an effort to avoid another barrage of comments.

Or they don't even read the comments and therefore learn nothing from the feedback. However, the major problem with the over-commented paper is that the instructor has lost both a sense of focus and a point of view.

The solution is to separate the mechanical comments and the substantive comments. The mechanical comments encourage the student to see the paper as a fixed piece that just needs some editing. The substantive comments, however, suggest that the student still needs to develop the meaning by doing more research.

When commenting on students' papers, think of your audience and your purpose. Your job as an instructor is to reach your students to help them learn and grow. If your comments do not accomplish your goal, then it doesn't matter how much time and effort you put into the papers.

Reprinted from *The Teaching Professor*, 23.8 (2009): 6.

Two Reasons I Still Use Rubrics

By Kevin Brown, Lee University, Tennessee

I began using grading rubrics for essays several years ago, and I was initially rather unhappy with how they worked. I found I was giving grades that I wouldn't have given when I graded without the rubric. Often the grades were higher, but not always. I gave enough lower grades to cause me to notice those as well.

Furthermore, using rubrics did not save me time in grading as they had been promised to do. I still wrote ample comments on the paper as I was reading it. However, I decided to stick with the rubrics, and I now understand why I had trouble at the beginning. I'd like to offer two reasons why I'm now in favor of using rubrics.

First, rubrics help students understand what is truly important in writing essays for my classes, which is especially helpful for students in the several sections of first-year composition that I teach every semester. Our students come from a wide variety of backgrounds, including those who've taken multiple AP English courses and those who readily admit that they've never written an academic essay. The rubric, especially when paired with sample essays from previous semesters, helps them see what I value in essays.

The rubric also identifies what I do not value, and that includes some aspects of papers that have counted for a significant portion of their grade previously. For example, many students have had teachers who were obsessed with the works cited page or with particular format issues. They tell me about teachers who would take off a point for every punctuation mark that was incorrect on the works cited page or teachers who measured margins and counted off points for the wrong formatting.

When they look at my rubric, they see that there is no section for formatting at all (though I certainly mark their mistakes), and the section on citations makes up only 10 percent of their grade and includes in-text citations as well as the works cited page.

Instead, they see that thesis, evidence, and structure count for 60 to 70 percent of their grade, depending on the paper. Add another 10 percent for their rough draft and peer editing, as I want them to learn the importance of writing multiple drafts and revising as part of a community, and there's not much left.

The rubric offers a visual representation of my definition of academic writing: thesis-driven and evidence-based. If my students have lost points on their papers, they understand that they needed a more substantial argument and stronger evidence to support it, not a different margin or more commas.

Oddly enough, the second reason I still use rubrics relates to the grading problems I had with them at the beginning. What I have found is that using rubrics reminds me of what I really believe is important in essays. Students often accuse professors of grading subjectively, and sometimes they're right. However, rubrics keep me focused on what I have told the students is actually important for the essay I am grading at the time.

It is too easy to see an essay with a good deal of red ink and give it a low grade, even if those red marks are evidence of a few minor errors that the student repeated throughout the paper. When guided by the need to mark a rubric, I am forced to look at my own description of a C thesis and see if that was honestly the problem with the essay or if the mistake was something less serious but persistent.

Also, when I am marking the essay as I read it, I am aware of what I need to circle on the rubric at the end. This guides my comments, making them more focused on the issues I have been teaching for the past few weeks. Instead of becoming frustrated because a student continues to use comma splices (even though I've yet to discuss them), I can help that student develop a clear thesis, something I have talked about and illustrated for several weeks but that he or she still does not yet seem to understand.

Since the rubric keeps me focused on the two or three issues I say I am most concerned about, we spend more class time discussing those issues.

In the end, the grades ultimately sorted themselves out as I have focused more time in class on issues that I really believe are important. Students write, understanding what is important, and that helps them improve in those areas. This should be the way grading works—actually measuring what the professor deems most important in a course.

Reprinted from *The Teaching Professor,* 24.4 (2010): 1.

Rubrics: Worth Using?

By Maryellen Weimer, Penn State Berks, Pennsylvania

Use of rubrics in higher education is comparatively recent. These grading aids that communicate "expectations for an assignment by listing the criteria or what counts, and describing levels of quality from excellent to poor" (p. 435) are being used to assess a variety of assignments such as literature reviews, reflective writings, bibliographies, oral presentations, critical thinking, portfolios, and projects. They are also being used across a range of disciplines, but so far the number of faculty using them remains small.

This background is provided in an excellent article that examines the "type and extent of empirical research on rubrics at the post-secondary level" and seeks "to stimulate research on rubric use in post-secondary teaching." (p. 437) A review of the literature on rubrics produced 20 articles, which are analyzed in this review.

So far, rubrics in higher education are being used almost exclusively as grading tools, even though some educators, like these authors, see them as having formative potential. When rubrics are given to students at the time an assignment is made, students can use them to better understand expectations for the assignment and then monitor and regulate their work.

They also make the grading process more transparent. In fact, in one of the studies analyzed in the review, one group of students were given the rubric after their work had been graded and another group got the rubric at the time the assignment was made. Both groups wanted to use rubrics again, but the rubric was rated as useful by 88 percent of the students who got it when the assignment was made as compared with 10 percent who rated it useful when it was returned with their graded assignment.

"One striking difference between students' and instructors' perceptions of rubric use is related to their perceptions of the purposes of rubrics. Students frequently referred to them as serving the purposes of learning and achievement, while instructors focused almost exclusively on the role of a rubric in quickly, objectively, and accurately assigning grades." (p. 439)

For teachers who might be considering use of rubrics or using them as something more than a time-saving grading mechanism, the key question is whether rubrics promote learning and achievement. The authors of this review found the evidence inconclusive. One study did find that involving students in developing and using rubrics prior to submitting an assignment was associated with improved academic performance, but another study found no differences in the quality of work done by students with and without rubrics.

Also missing from the research so far are answers to questions related to validity and reliability. Do rubrics measure what they purport to measure—the validity question? "A large majority of the studies reviewed did not describe the process of development of rubrics to establish their quality." (p. 445)

A bit more work has been done on reliability, and it shows that with training, separate raters consistently give similar ratings to a piece of work when using the same rubric. However, the authors note that more work on rubric validity and reliability is needed.

Are rubrics worth using? Research answers to the question are still few and not always conclusive. Among practitioners, there is general agreement that rubrics do expedite the grading process and make it seem more objective and fair to students. Among students, there is agreement that rubrics clarify expectations and are especially useful as they prepare assignments.

The researchers recommend "educating instructors on the formative use of rubrics to promote learning by sharing or co-creating them with students in order to make the goals and qualities of an assignment transparent, and to have students use rubrics to guide peer and self-assessment and subsequent revision." (p. 444)

Reference: Reddy, Y. M., and Andrade, H. (2010). "A review of rubric use in higher education." *Assessment & Evaluation in Higher Education, 35 (4), 435–448.*

Reprinted from *The Teaching Professor*, 26.1 (2012): 4.

Quick Feedback, Engaged Students

By Kevin Brown, Lee University, Tennessee

We often wonder what we can do to help students engage with the material so they can learn it at a deeper level. Students don't make that an easy task. They arrive in class having not read the material or having not thought about it in meaningful ways, and that keeps them from being engaged in class.

Several years ago, I read George Kuh's article "What Student Engagement Data Tell Us about College Readiness," in which he writes, "Students who talk about substantive matters with faculty and peers, are challenged to perform at high levels, and *receive frequent feedback* on their performance typically get better grades, are more satisfied with college, and are more likely to persist." (*Peer Review*, January 1, 2007, p. 4; italics mine).

Here are three ways I try to provide feedback that engages students and not overwhelm myself with grading tasks in the process.

Short essays: Whenever I mention essays to colleagues, they worry that I am suggesting they spend every weekend reading papers. I have found two shorter assignments that help students and me know whether they understand the material and that can be graded quickly. The note-card essay limits student responses to a 3x5 or 4x6 card. One of my colleagues has his upper-level students create a question and then write a response to it. He uses the questions and answers on their cards to stimulate discussion in class. He finds that doing so draws out students who don't often speak in class.

Also, I use one-page essays that focus on a single skill or idea, a technique I stole from Irvin Hashimoto's *Thirteen Weeks*. In my freshman composition course, I assign several of these essays, but I grade them only for thesis and evidence (or whatever skill I'm having students practice). In a sophomore literature survey, they focus on one idea, such as reason or passion in *The Enlightenment*. Even in junior-level literature courses, the students respond to a quote from a critic, giving them practice at integrating and responding to quotations in their writing. Doing so helps them avoid the random sprinkling of quotations throughout their longer papers.

Online forums: Most college and university computer systems include some sort of forum or blog capability. We use Moodle, where I can set up a forum for students to post to and respond. In my upper-division courses, students post 150- to 250-word responses to the assigned readings. These responses are long enough to encourage interaction with the text but not so long that it takes me more than 20 to 30 minutes to read an entire class's responses.

Like my colleague, I use their responses to provoke class discussion. Having written a response, most students come to that discussion with an idea already in mind. This encourages those reluctant to participate to offer ideas and insights.

These online forums have other benefits as well. First, I do not have to spend class time on ideas students already understand. Since I read their posts before class, I can see that 15 or 20 of them have all commented on an idea I had planned to discuss. When it's clear they understand the idea, I mention it briefly in class, praising them for recognizing its importance, and then I move on to some idea not discussed in their posts.

If their responses contain evidence that they are confused about or misunderstanding an idea, I can address that in class. When I mention that several posts indicated confusion about an issue, students see that they weren't the only ones not understanding something in the reading. Sometimes I intervene in the forum, offering clarification, but I still spend time on the idea in class to make sure it is clear.

Process writing: We tend to talk about the writing process only in freshman composition courses. However, using the process in all disciplines—where students sequentially turn in an annotated bibliography and rough draft, go through peer editing and conferences with professors, and then turn in a final draft—gives them consistent feedback throughout the process.

They produce better papers as a result. You can help them deepen their thinking as they work on the paper. You can catch writing and bibliography problems and can raise questions about content that may be plagiarized. Talking with students about their topics and reading bibliographies is not time-consuming, and taking such steps makes the writing process a richer learning experience. If they submit better papers, that speeds up the grading process at the end of the course.

Students are more likely to be engaged in classes when they receive regular feedback. It keeps them on track. Shorter assignments, technology, and process writing can help engage students, leading to better discussions and more complex thinking, and those results benefit students and teachers.

Reprinted from *The Teaching Professor,* 26.9 (2012): 1.

Chapter 3:
Grading Participation

How Accurately Do Students Track Their Participation?

By Maryellen Weimer, Penn State-Berks, Pennsylvania

Grading participation presents a number of challenges. If instructors rely on their sense of who participated, how often, and in what ways, that can be a pretty subjective measure. After all, besides noting who's contributing, the instructor needs to listen to what the student is saying and frame a response while keeping the larger discussion context in mind.

Is the discussion staying on track? Are there points that have yet to be made? If instructors opt for a more objective system, they face the cumbersome task of comment counting during the actual discussion. While listening to the student, the instructor must find the student's name and record the comment. It requires a challenging set of multitasking skills.

What about letting students keep track of their participation? Probably not a good idea if that participation is graded. Do they overrate their participation? Yes, they do, according to several studies. But a recent study used a different approach to having students track their contributions and found that they did not overrate their contributions.

These students in three sections of the same undergraduate human development course (there were between 51 and 57 of them in each section) were instructed in the syllabus to write a phrase or a sentence to describe each comment they made during designated discussion periods in the class.

Comments that could be counted included asking a question, answering a question, or sharing an opinion about an issue being discussed. Students recorded their comments on cards provided by the instructor, and students gave those cards to graduate teaching assistants at the end of each period. Students recorded their comments on 20 discussion days. They received two points for the first comment made in class and one for the second, for a maximum of three points per day. Participation credit counted for 4 percent of the total course grade.

Unbeknownst to the students, the graduate students observing in the class on the 20 discussion days recorded student contributions on five of those days. Students were not told what the graduate students were doing in the class.

The researchers explain, "The range of student-observer correlations across all sections and units proved to be 0.71 to 0.95. . . . These correlations were not significantly different ($p = 0.19$)." (p. 44) By statistical measures, the correlations were large, with 95 percent of them 0.80 or greater.

The researchers also wondered how accurate student reports of their participation would be on those days when participation was not graded. Some earlier research reported that in this case, students underreported their participation, and that was confirmed in this study as well.

Based on their findings, this faculty research team recommends having students keep track of their participation using this approach. "Writing one's specific comments on an official record card [provides] a more accurate basis for determining participation credit. Assigning participation credit by using this technique would help assure students of a fair assessment." (p. 45) They also say that the system is manageable in classes of this size. In larger classes, students could be divided into subsets, with each subset earning credit on a designated day.

Reference: Kroch, K. B., Foster, L. N., McCleary, D. F., Aspiranti, K. B., Nalls, M. L., Quillivan, C. C., Taylor, C. M., and Williams, R. L. (2011). "Reliability of students' self-recorded participation in class discussion." *Teaching of Psychology, 38* (1), 43–45.

Reprinted from *The Teaching Professor*, 25.9 (2011): 2.

Assessing Class Participation: One Useful Strategy

By Denise D. Knight, SUNY Cortland, New York

One of the changes we have seen in academia in the last 30 years or so is the shift from lecture-based classes to courses that encourage a student-centered approach. Few instructors would quibble with the notion that promoting active participation helps students think critically and argue more effectively.

However, even the most savvy instructors are still confounded about how to best evaluate participation, particularly when it is graded along with more traditional assessment measures, such as essays, exams, and oral presentations. Type the words "class participation" and "assessment" into www.google.com, and you will get close to 700,000 hits.

Providing students with a clear, fair, and useful assessment of their class participation is challenging for even the most seasoned educator. Even when I provide a rubric that distinguishes every category of participation from outstanding to poor, students are often still confused about precisely what it is that I expect from them.

It is not unusual, for example, for students to believe that attendance and participation are synonymous. On the other hand, when we attempt to spell out too precisely what it is we expect in the way of contributions, we run the risk of closing down participation.

In one online site that offers assessment guidelines, for example, the course instructor characterizes "unsatisfactory" participation as follows: "Contributions in class reflect inadequate preparation. Ideas offered are seldom substantive, provide few if any insights and never a constructive direction for the class. Integrative comments and effective challenges are absent. If this person were not a member of the class, valuable airtime would be saved."

The language used in the description—"inadequate," "seldom," "few," "never," and "absent"—hardly encourages positive results. The final sentence is both dismissive and insensitive. Shy students are unlikely to risk airing an opinion in a classroom climate that is negatively charged.

Certainly, the same point can be made by simply informing students in writing that infrequent contributions to class discussions will be deemed unsatisfactory and merit a D for the participation grade.

While there are a number of constructive guidelines online for generating and assessing participation, the dichotomy between the students' perception of their contributions and the instructor's assessment of participation is still often a problem.

One tool that I have found particularly effective is to administer a brief questionnaire early in the semester (as soon as I have learned everyone's name) that asks students to assess their own participation to date. Specifically, I ask that students do the following: "Please check the statement below that best corresponds to your honest assessment of your contribution to class discussion thus far:

_____ I contribute several times during every class discussion. (A)
_____ I contribute at least once during virtually every class discussion. (B)
_____ I often contribute to class discussion. (C)
_____ I occasionally contribute to class discussion. (D)
_____ I rarely contribute to class discussion. (E)"

I then provide a space on the form for the students to write a brief rationale for their grade, along with the option to write additional comments if they so choose. Finally, I include a section on the form for instructor response. I collect the forms, read them, offer a brief response, and return them at the next class meeting.

This informal self-assessment exercise does not take long, and it always provides intriguing results. More often than not, students will award themselves a higher participation grade than I would have. Their rationale often yields insight into why there is a disconnect between my perception and theirs.

For example, a student may write, "I feel that I have earned a B so far in class participation. I know that I'm quiet, but I haven't missed a class and I always do my reading." Using the "Instructor Response" space, I now have an opportunity to disabuse the student's notion that preparation, attendance, and participation are one and the same. I also offer concrete measures that the student can take to improve his or her participation.

When this exercise is done early in the semester, it can enhance both the amount and quality of participation. It helps to build confidence and reminds students that they have to hold themselves accountable for every part of their course grade, including participation.

Reprinted from *The Teaching Professor,* 21.3 (2007): 1.

Teaching How to Question: Participation Rubrics

By Anna H. Lathrop, Brock University, Ontario, Canada

At the heart of the Socratic method—the icon of the inquiry-based learn-ing approach—is the art of asking the "right" question. Indeed, when we engage in casual conversation with friends, our dialogue is often ani-mated and enjoyable—interspersed with questions that force us to engage in a spontaneous and free-flowing exchange of knowledge, ideas, and reflec-tion.

In an educational context, however, without the markers of personal fa-miliarity and natural interest, the institutional forum of the "seminar" often feels foreign, stilted, and intimidating.

After years of teaching large first-year classes with multiple seminar sec-tions and a cohort of new TA seminar leaders each year, I have developed two evaluation rubrics. One is designed to assess student participation, and the other aims to assess student facilitation. Both follow this article.

In each case, principles that relate to the skills of asking good questions are embedded within evaluation rubrics. Their presence helps both frame and assess the teaching and learning environment of the seminar.

Students are assessed on a weekly basis with the participation rubric and are assigned a value out of 20 marks for each seminar. These values are aver-aged over the 12-week term to yield an average seminar performance rating. This rating is converted to a value of 20 percent of their final grade.

During the course of the term, each student is also asked to facilitate a seminar on a given topic (with a partner, if desired). The facilitation evalua-tion also consists of five levels of assessment with qualitative ratings and cor-responding numeric values. This assessment is marked out of 20 and converted to a value of 5 percent of the final grade in the course. Seminars range in number from 15 to 20 students.

These evaluation rubrics grew out of my belief that the seminar is a critical component of inquiry-based learning. In this forum for immediate interpersonal interaction, students benefit from the opportunity to ask questions, observe the enabling effect of these questions on others, and assess the overall impact of this exchange of ideas in the teaching and learning context.

Students must have the opportunity to both participate and facilitate in this academic exchange with clear and explicit criteria for excellence. In an age when PowerPoint presentations prevail in classrooms, the art of spontaneous, interactive, face-to-face dialogue that teaches students how to question and respond in the seminar environment is imperative.

Editor's note: The author has graciously granted permission for faculty to reproduce these rubrics for use in class without requesting permission. In all other cases, permission to reprint the rubrics must be requested from Magna Publications, following the standard protocols.

Seminar Participation Evaluation
Rating: Poor = 1, Satisfactory = 2, Very Good = 3, Superior = 4

Student Name	Preparation • Evidence shows preparation for the seminar (has prepared notes and/or recalls the readings without the use of the open text).	Engagement • Quality of engagement is active, respectful & inclusive.	Initiative • Questions asked focus, clarify & summarize discussion.	Response • Quality of response reflects knowledge, comprehension & application of the readings.	Discussion • Quality of response extends the discussion with peers and reflects analysis, synthesis & evaluation.	Total /20
1						
2						
3						
4						
5						
6						

Anecdotal Comments: _____

Seminar Facilitation Evaluation

Student Facilitators: 1. _____ 2. _____ Date: _____

Rating: Poor = 1, Satisfactory = 2, Very Good = 3, Superior = 4

1. Facilitation Skills:
  • Facilitators ask questions and use   **(1)   (2)   (3)   (4)**
  strategies that draw out knowledge of
  theory/experience; facilitators are
  knowledgeable and offer correction &
  guidance when necessary.

2. Organization:
  • Seminar is structured in a clear   **(1)   (2)   (3)   (4)**
  & logical sequence.

3. Originality:
  • Visual and written aids are   **(1)   (2)   (3)   (4)**
  interesting, innovative/creative
  & helpful.

4. Engagement:
  • Facilitators generate a high degree   **(1)   (2)   (3)   (4)**
  of student interest; respectful &
  inclusive; all students encouraged
  to participate.

4. Discussion:
  • Discussion is focused, relevant   **(1)   (2)   (3)   (4)**
  & engaging; theory (readings)
  related to experience; applications
  & implications clear and accurate.

TOTAL :   20 marks _____

**NOTE: Student co-facilitators may receive similar or different grades,
      depending upon their level of preparation and contribution.**

Reprinted from *The Teaching Professor,* 20.3 (2006): 4–5.

A Participation Rubric

By Adam Chapnick, University of Toronto, Ontario, Canada

After years of orally stating my expectations for tutorial participation, I have developed a rubric that I think both improves my accountability as an assessor while also providing my students with a clear sense of my expectations for class discussions. It also makes clear my focus in the small group setting: creating a "learners-centered," as opposed to a "learner-centered," environment.

The rubric is currently being used in a third-year Canadian external relations course. Tutorials are held biweekly and are made up of 12 to 15 students plus an instructor-facilitator. The students are assigned approximately four readings (60 to 80 pages) per session. The readings usually contain two opposing arguments on a Canadian foreign policy issue (for example, arguments for and against free trade) and approximately two pieces of primary evidence (House of Commons speeches, government documents, etc.).

On class participation

Unlike some of the other forms of learning that take place in this class, **participation in the small-group environment is not an individual activity.** How and what you learn from listening to a lecture, reading a textbook, doing research, or studying for an exam are quite different from what you can gain when you have immediate access to approximately 15 different, informed points of view on a single issue.

In tutorial, if you do not prepare effectively and contribute positively, other students miss out on one of those points of view, and their learning experience suffers. For this reason, **my evaluation of your performance in tutorial will be based in large part on how you have improved the learning experience of your peers.** Supporting, engaging, and listening to your peers does not mean that you must always agree with them. Rather, you should make a sincere effort to respond to their comments.

Playing an active role in discussions involves volunteering your opinion, asking questions, and listening carefully.

The best discussions are the ones that move beyond the simple questions and answers. You will be rewarded for bringing up more challenging ideas and for trying to deal with them collaboratively with your classmates. To do this effectively, you must have read all of the assigned material carefully. If you haven't, it will become clear quite quickly.

The following rubric sets out the criteria upon which you will be evaluated.

A guide to grading your class participation

A+

- Actively supports, engages, and listens to peers (ongoing);
- arrives fully prepared at every session;
- plays an active role in discussions (ongoing);
- comments advance the level and depth of the dialogue (consistently);
- *group dynamic and level of discussion are consistently better because of the student's presence*

A

- Actively supports, engages, and listens to peers (ongoing);
- arrives fully prepared at almost every session;
- plays an active role in discussions (ongoing);
- comments occasionally advance the level and depth of the dialogue;
- *group dynamic and level of discussion are often better because of the student's presence*

B

- Makes a sincere effort to interact with peers (ongoing);
- arrives mostly if not fully prepared (ongoing);
- participates constructively in discussions (ongoing);
- makes relevant comments based on the assigned material (ongoing);
- *group dynamic and level of discussion are occasionally better (never worse) because of the student's presence*

C

- Limited interaction with peers;
- preparation, and therefore level of participation, are both inconsistent;
- when prepared, participates constructively in discussions and makes relevant comments based on the assigned material;
- *group dynamic and level of discussion are not affected by the student's presence*

D

- Virtually no interaction with peers;
- rarely prepared;
- rarely participates;
- comments are generally vague or drawn from outside the assigned material;
- demonstrates a noticeable lack of interest (on occasion);
- *group dynamic and level of discussion are harmed by the student's presence*

F

- No interaction with peers;
- never prepared;
- never participates;
- demonstrates a noticeable lack of interest in the material (ongoing);
- *group dynamic and level of discussion are significantly harmed by the student's presence*

An explanation of this rubric and additional factors (such as attendance) that may affect your grade are discussed below.

Beyond the rubric

Additional factors that may affect your grade positively:

- If you show **measurable improvement** as the year goes on, you will be rewarded significantly. Becoming more active and/or making more effective comments not only raises the overall level of discussion in the room, but it also sets an example for the rest of the class. By trying, you encourage others to do the same.
- If you are naturally shy or have a day when you are not yourself, you may email me relevant comments, thoughts, and questions after the discussion. While this method of participation is not ideal (it does not engage the rest of the group), it does demonstrate that you have been preparing for the class, listening carefully, and responding to your peers.
- If you miss a session completely, you can submit a one-page (single-spaced) typed **argumentative summary** of the assigned material. (This means you must analyze and critique the readings, not summarize them.) Again, while not ideal, this will confirm that you have engaged and responded to the material.

Additional factors that may affect your grade negatively:

- **Not attending tutorial will have a significant impact on your final grade (regardless of the quality of your contributions during weeks when you are there).** Obviously, you cannot contribute if you are absent. More important, not attending sets a poor example for your peers and encourages them to do the same. Finally, a cohesive and supportive class dynamic is most easily developed and maintained in a relatively predictable and consistent environment. Your peers must know you and trust you to feel comfortable; it is much more difficult to build this trust if you do not attend tutorial regularly.

- Dominating class discussions is not helpful. It denies other students the opportunity to contribute and therefore restricts the number of ideas that might be considered. Dominating also prevents you from listening and from building effectively on the comments of your peers.

- Speaking directly to the teaching assistant/tutorial leader is also highly discouraged. Tutorial is supposed to be a dialogue among peers, not a series of individual one-on-one conversations. Ignoring your peers— and/or not referring to them by name—risks alienating them and creates a much less supportive group dynamic.

- Negative, offensive, and disrespectful comments and actions can do serious damage to the learning atmosphere. Such behavior will necessarily result in a substantially lower grade.

Editor's note: When we publish materials that instructors use in classes, we ask them to grant other instructors permission to use these materials in their courses. Professor Chapnick has given this permission. Please note this is permission for classroom use only. Permission to reprint the rubric elsewhere must be requested through normal channels.

Reprinted from *The Teaching Professor*, 19.3 (2005): 4.

Evaluating Online Discussions

By Maryellen Weimer, Penn State-Berks, Pennsylvania

Discussion in class and online are not the same. When a comment is keyed in, more time can be involved in deciding what will be said. Online comments have more permanence. They can be read more than once and responded to more specifically. Online commentary isn't delivered orally and evokes fewer of the fears associated with speaking in public.

These features begin the list of what makes online discussions different. These different features also have implications for how online exchanges are assessed. What evaluation criteria are appropriate?

Two researchers offer data helpful in answering the assessment question. They decided to take a look at a collection of rubrics being used to assess online discussions. They analyzed 50 rubrics they found online by using various search engines and keywords.

All the rubrics in this sample were developed to assess online discussions in higher education, and they did so with 153 different performance criteria. Based on a keyword analysis, the researchers grouped this collection into four major categories. Each is briefly discussed here.

Cognitive criteria—Forty-four percent of the criteria were assigned to this category, which loosely represented the caliber of the intellectual thinking displayed by the student in the online exchange. Many of the criteria emphasized critical thinking, problem solving and argumentation, knowledge construction, creative thinking, and course content and readings.

Many also attempted to assess the extent to which the thinking was deep and not superficial. Others looked at the student's ability "to apply, explain and interpret information; to use inferences; provide conclusions; and suggest solutions." (p. 812)

Mechanical criteria—Almost 20 percent of the criteria were assigned to this category. These criteria essentially assessed the student's writing ability, including use of language, grammatical and spelling correctness, organization, writing style, and the use of references and citations. "Ratings that stress clarity ... benefit other learners by allowing them to concentrate on the message rather than spend their time trying to decipher unclear messages." (p. 813)

However, the authors worry that the emphasis on the mechanical aspects of language may detract from the student's ability to contribute in-depth analysis and reflection. They note the need for more research about the impact of this group of assessment criteria.

Procedural/managerial criteria—The criteria in this group focused on the students' contributions and conduct in the online exchange environment. Almost 19 percent of the criteria belonged to this category. More specifically, these criteria dealt with the frequency of and timeliness of the postings. Others assessed the degree of respect and the extent to which students adhered to specified rules of conduct.

Interactive criteria—About 18 percent of the criteria were placed in this category, and they assessed the degree to which students reacted to and interacted with each other. Were students responding to what others said, answering the questions of others, and asking others questions? Were they providing feedback? Were they using the contributions of others in their comments?

This work is not prescriptive. It does not propose which criteria are right or best. However, it does give teachers a good sense of those aspects of online interaction that are most regularly being assessed, which can be helpful in creating or revising a set of assessment criteria.

Beyond what others are using, a teacher's decision should be guided by the goals and objectives of an online discussion activity. What does the teacher aspire for students to know and to be able to do as a result of interacting with others in an online exchange?

Reference: Penny, L. and Murphy, E. (2009). "Rubrics for designing and evaluating online asynchronous discussions." *British Journal of Educational Technology,* 40 (5), 804–820.

Reprinted from *The Teaching Professor,* 27.3 (2013): 6.

Chapter 4:
Talking with Students about Grades

Conversations about Grades: Realistic Expectations

By Maryellen Weimer, Penn State-Berks, Pennsylvania

What instructor has not been stressed and disappointed by a student with a grade issue? So many students seem so ready to blame their poor performances on everybody and everything else. It's as if they have no responsibility at all for the grades they have received. And then there's the student who debates an answer and in the process seems genuinely interested in the content. But the truth comes out as the conversation concludes: "Well, do I get credit for this answer or not?"

Clearly there are no easy answers or simple solutions that reliably make conversations about grades constructive learning experiences. And there are not any contained in the research referenced below. However, this study does offer some insights that can help an instructor better understand and be more realistic about grade conversations with students.

Don't harbor any illusions about the primary goals of these conversations. Researchers hypothesized that students might have one of three goals for the conversation. They might be interested in **learning**, as in better understanding the material or the reason why they did so poorly so that future performances might improve.

Or students might have the goal of **persuading** the instructor to change the low grades to higher ones. Here the conversation is one of negotiation as the student tries for more points or a grade-level change.

Finally, the goal for students may be **fighting.** Because students are often emotionally involved with their grades and experience frustration and anger when they receive low ones, they may decide to vent their feelings to the instructor.

A sample of 234 students were asked to "consider a recent conversation in which you talked with one of your instructors about a grade on an assignment that you felt was lower than you desired." Among other things, they were asked to describe that conversation, identify their goals for it, and say what they thought caused the grade and whether they were satisfied with the outcome of the conversation.

As for their goals, 66 percent had "persuading the instructor to change the grade" as their primary goal. Only 9 percent stated learning goals and 8 percent reported goals that equated with fighting. Another small category of students reported goals that related to impressing the instructor.

Consistent with these goals, students reported outcomes related to whether or not the grades were changed. A surprising 41 percent reported that their grades were changed and so they were satisfied with the outcomes. Only 14 percent did not mention grades in their responses to an open-ended question about conversation outcomes.

These researchers also explored relationships between conversation goals and the causes to which students attributed their low grades. As might be suspected, this research confirmed that students who listed learning goals were most likely to attribute the causes to reasons within themselves, whereas students with fighting goals attributed the poor performance to causes beyond their control.

Also, if students had the goal of persuading, fighting, or impressing, they were less polite and more likely to use messages aimed at causing the instructor to lose face. ("You were never explicitly clear" or "I think I was marked down a bit too harshly on this problem.")

Some of the practitioner literature suggests that grade conflicts can be avoided by sharing grading rubrics with students before they complete assignments, even giving students a role in creating those rubrics or otherwise letting them participate in the grading process.

However, these findings do not lead to a lot of optimism about the effectiveness of these strategies or any others in decreasing the number of complaints about grades. "There were few students in this sample who had never had a conflict about grades." (p. 201) Students continue to be very grade-oriented.

Although this research did not report positive findings related to the goals students have for these conversations or the communication strategies they are inclined to use to achieve their desired outcomes, it is helpful that an instructor be able to understand where a student is coming from in the conversation.

Instructors should not respond emotionally even when students use strategies designed to impugn them. Who was to blame for the poor performance? Instructors are certainly not absolved of responsibility, but more often than not it is student behaviors that account for a less-than-lovely grade. Instructors also need to think clearly about when and under what conditions they change grades.

And in any student-initiated conversation about a grade, the learning question is appropriate to ask. "So, have you learned anything through this experience that might be important to remember as you continue this course and your education?"

Reference: Sabee, C.M. and Wilson, S.R. (2005). "Students' primary goals, attributions, and facework during conversations about disappointing grades." *Communication Education,* 54 (3), 185–204.

Reprinted from *The Teaching Professor,* 20.3 (2006): 5.

Teachable Moments:
The Grading Conference

By Bill Latham, US Army Command and General Staff College, Fort Leaven-worth, Kansas

Grading student papers may be the college instructor's least pleasant duty. Most of us carefully mark each page, noting problems, questioning assumptions, and offering additional information, many times on the final version of the essay when it is too late to make improvements. I have colleagues who spend up to an hour on each paper, despite the distinct possibility that their feedback may not even be read, much less understood.

Still, careful and thoughtful grading is worth our time and effort. Students deserve feedback on the quality of their ideas and the clarity of their writing, if only to hear a different perspective, and certainly to improve their next written assignment. Although I try to achieve these goals with my marginal notes and end comments on every paper, I rarely find out whether these comments helped.

However, things change considerably when I deliver my feedback in person. I invite my students to sit with me while I grade their papers. These voluntary "grading conferences" achieve three mutually beneficial goals.

First, the conferences expedite the assessment process, satisfying students' anxiety about their grades, and at the same time they force me to overcome the urge to procrastinate. To this end, I frequently invite students to schedule grading appointments with me immediately after turning in their assignments. The sooner I provide feedback, the sooner they can incorporate my observations into their next effort. For my part, the more writing conferences I can accomplish on the day of turn-in, the fewer papers left to grade.

Second, these personal conferences allow for clarification. They give students the opportunity to clarify ambiguous claims, explain disjointed arguments, and identify elusive thesis statements, while I gain the chance to not only ask what my students meant but also to hear their answers. I take as much interest in what they think as how they think, and I want them to know how the tone of their arguments and the quality of their evidence influences their audience.

Finally, grading conferences improve the quality of my feedback to students. In person, I can show them specific ways to improve their writing, and their verbal and nonverbal cues tell me whether they understand my comments. When they don't understand, I can find other ways to illustrate my point, and they in turn have the chance to ask me what I mean.

Grading conferences do have limitations. For one thing, they consume more of my own time and effort than simply grading in private. Conferences also require students to invest more time and energy in assignments they have already completed. In addition, some students may object strongly to my assessment, argue with every suggestion for improvement, or seize the opportunity to negotiate for a higher grade.

Occasionally, students attend merely to humor me, stoically accepting my comments as if the conference were a trial to be endured. As these situations are generally unpleasant for both parties concerned, attendance at my conferences is voluntary.

Despite these risks, I continue to invite and encourage students to sit with me while I grade their papers. Successful conferences enable us to reach a mutual appreciation of what did and didn't work in a specific piece of writing. The student leaves with a grade, a clear understanding of why it was assigned, and one or more strategies for achieving better results.

Occasionally, I get to look a student in the eye, praise the excellence of his or her work, and affirm that it is as good as or better than I could have done with the same assignment.

The main benefit, however, is better writing. The grading conference provides a great opportunity to move toward that goal. Students deserve our feedback on the quality of their ideas and the clarity of their writing. I find that such feedback has its greatest impact when delivered in person, where such exchanges create that most rare and precious of opportunities in a college course—the teachable moment.

Reprinted from *The Teaching Professor*, 25.7 (2011): 1.

The "I Deserve a Better Grade on This" Conversation

By Maryellen Weimer, Penn State-Berks, Pennsylvania

It's a conversation most faculty would rather not have. The student is unhappy about a grade on a paper, project, or exam or for the course. It's also a conversation most students would rather not have. In the study referenced below, only 16.8 percent of students who reported they had received a grade other than what they thought their work deserved actually went to see the professor to discuss the grade.

Even though faculty might not want to increase the number of grade conversations they have with students, there is an interesting question here. Why didn't more students come to talk about the grade they didn't think they deserved? Maybe they really didn't have a problem with the grade but only wished they had done better.

That might be true for some students, but this study tested (and verified) two theoretical frameworks that identify some of what makes these conversations difficult for students. They need to persuade the teacher, who has complete control over the grade, to change his or her mind—the grade decision has already been made, and most teachers feel some pressure to defend their decisions. Teachers also know how badly students want good grades whether they deserve them or not.

According to the theories that this research attempted to test, students must also behave in a socially appropriate way or they risk jeopardizing their overall relationship with the teacher, which may influence the grades they receive on subsequent assignments.

One would hope that experience and maturity would enable teachers to maintain their objectivity, but students are often personally vested in their grades and are not always sophisticated communicators. They may be defensive and angry and unfairly accuse the teacher. Most of us have had a few conversations like this, which is why most of us would rather not discuss contested grades with students.

But these exchanges can be moments of learning for students and teachers, and they need to be thought of in that way. Teachers need to begin by listening to student objections and concerns about the grade. If it's a case of "you don't understand how hard I worked on this paper," it's an opportunity to discuss how difficult it is for teachers to assess effort and how grades are more about performance than effort.

It's also an opportunity to ascertain whether the student understands the feedback that has been provided. Can he or she read the teacher's comments? Does the student understand how and why the partial credit is awarded? If a problem is persistent through the performance, can the student identify unmarked examples of it?

It's possible the grade should be changed. Teachers need to have these conversations recognizing that grading (especially lots of it) is not an infallible process. It is probably best to let the student make the case for the change, ascertain whether the feedback provided is correctly understood, but defer the decision to change or not change the grade until the work can be reviewed without the student sitting across the desk.

The learning potential of these conversations is a function of how forward-looking they are. "So, what have you learned from this experience that will help you with the next assignment?" "What are you going to work on?" Here, depending on the student, it might be wise for the teacher to provide some guidance. "Let me identify three things to work on. All three would significantly improve the quality of your work, and if there is improvement in these areas, that will definitely be reflected in your grade."

If the student has conducted himself or herself appropriately in the conversation, that deserves a comment. "I appreciate the maturity you've demonstrated in this conversation, and although I'm sure you're disappointed that I haven't changed my mind about your grade on this paper, I do think these conversations are very important."

And they are important. Teachers need to know when a student thinks a grade is unfair. They need to review their decisions, and they need to try to help the student understand why the grade stands.

How do teachers make it more likely that students will discuss concerns about grades and discuss them constructively? Teachers talk more about the importance of these conversations. They invite students to come to the office to talk about grades the students don't think they deserve. They explain why these conversations are challenging for students and teachers, and they give students good advice about what to say and not say about the grade they want changed.

Whether you're the teacher or the student, these aren't easy conversations. It's not in either party's interest to back down. But that need to defend a position should not become an obstacle that compromises what both parties can learn from these conversations.

Reference: Henningsen, M.L.M., Valde, K.S., Russell, G.A., and Russell, G.R. (2011). "Student-faculty interactions about disappointing grades: Application of the Goals—Plans—Actions Model and the Theory of Planned Behavior." *Communication Education*, 60 (2), 174–190.

Reprinted from *The Teaching Professor*, 26.2 (2012): 3.

Giving Students Choices in How Much Assignments Count

By Maryellen Weimer, Penn State-Berks, Pennsylvania

Grades often get in the way of learning even though they are supposed to do just the opposite. When students get fixated on their grades, learning takes a back seat. How can instructors deal with the importance of grades and simultaneously use them for their other intended purpose—to promote learning?

Some have proposed this idea: give students a certain amount of choice regarding the weight of assignments. This strategy allows students to select assignments that are of greater interest; if an assignment is perceived as more interesting, more learning might be the result.

Giving students a choice also allows them to select learning experiences they prefer or ones that correspond to their strengths as learners. Said another way, when students have a choice, they have some control over what and how they study.

These were some of the reasons that motivated research that involved letting MBA students designate (within ranges) the weight of certain assignments. Specifically, they could decide how much three assignments would count in their final grade calculation: class participation, a case analysis paper, and a final group project.

Students could allocate between a minimum of 15 percent and a maximum of 45 percent of their final grade to each of these assignments, provided the total allocated did not exceed 75 percent of the final course grade. In the control sections, each of these assignments counted for 25 percent of the course grade. Students made these allocations during the third week of the semester, and once made they could not be changed.

Students given this weighting choice and those not given the choice were surveyed at the end of the course. Sixty-seven percent of the students in the choice sections indicated they would like to designate assignment weights in other courses. Several different comparisons showed a higher level of interest in the course expressed by students given this choice than by students unable to change assignment weights.

Students given the choice also indicated greater interest in taking subsequent courses in the content area. End-of-course student ratings underscored these results. "Students in the choice condition rated the course higher on 30 out of 36 items relative to the non-choice conditions." (p. 270)

Several other results were interesting. For example, on average students weighted the assignments very close to the default grading scheme of 25 percent for each assignment: 24.2 percent for participation (SD of 6.8 percent and a range of 15 to 45 percent), 25.8 percent for the case analysis paper (SD of 5.3 percent and a range of 15 to 35 percent), and 25 percent for the final group project (SD of 5.4 percent and a range of 15 to 35 percent). Almost 20 percent of the students simply chose the default scheme.

Why were these students afraid to have one assignment count significantly more or less than another? Did they think that would jeopardize their course grade? The researchers observe, "This suggests that students may have been unwilling to accept or leverage the choice offered to them and instead used a risk-averse strategy." (p. 270)

Perhaps even more intriguing is the finding that students given this choice did not earn course grades higher than those not given the choice. "The choice intervention had no impact on the total points student earned in the course." (p. 267)

So if grades measure learning, then students given the option of weighting assignments differently did not learn more even though their interest in the course and subsequent ones was significantly higher. The researchers do note in discussing the practical implications of their research that their goal was to keep the choice and non-choice settings as similar as possible, and so they did not talk about the choice option in those sections or integrate it further into the course design. They recommend doing both in non-research settings.

Is this strategy a way to get students focused a bit more on learning and a bit less on just getting the grade? It may be, but these findings would seem to indicate that students need teachers to help them understand what can be learned by making these choices.

Reference: Dobrow, S.R., Smith, W.K., and Posner, M.A. (2011). "Managing the grading paradox: Leveraging the power of choice in the classroom."

Academy of Management Learning & Education, 10 (2), 261–276.

Reprinted from *The Teaching Professor,* 26.6 (2012): 5.

Do Students Really Know Their Academic Strengths?

By Brian A. Vander Schee, Aurora University, Illinois

Students focus on grades far more so than faculty would like. This is particularly true when students do not receive the grades they believe they deserve. They think that some assignments disadvantage them—they don't do well on essay exams or don't want to work with others in groups. I wondered how students would respond if they were given the opportunity to select the weight distribution for graded course components. The assignments would be preset, clearly described in the course syllabus, and students would complete each one, but they could select the percentage of their grade accounted for by each assignment.

This is exactly the approach I took in two sections of the Capstone: Strategic Management course. Students were given a grading agreement on the first day of class that asked them to select one of the designated percentage weights for each assignment that I would use in calculating their final course grade. I would now recommend letting the students have until the second week of class to finalize their decisions. They need time to get acquainted with the course and find out about their assignments in other courses.

The four graded components in the course included (1) case preparation and class participation (10 percent, 15 percent, or 20 percent); (2) individual written case analyses (30 percent, 35 percent, 40 percent, 45 percent, 50 percent, 55 percent, or 60 percent); (3) group case presentation (10 percent, 15 percent, or 20 percent); and (4) business strategy game (15 percent, 20 percent, 25 percent, 30 percent, or 35 percent). Once their choices were submitted, students were not permitted to make any changes to their designated distribution.

Students submitted a written rationale explaining how they decided on their particular distribution. Most said they chose the assignments they thought maximized their strengths as learners (53.8 percent) or they decreased the value of assignments that required skills they considered weaknesses (30.8 percent).

I solicited feedback from them about this approach at the end of the course, and most students were satisfied with the process. Comments like these were common: "I felt more in control." "My grade was in my own hands." "It gave me more self-confidence." Students perceived that they had more control over their final grade, and this perception motivated them to engage in the learning process.

I was curious whether students really knew their academic strengths. If they did, their final grades would be higher than when I set the assignment percentages. However, the actual manipulation of the percentages did not determine how well students performed in the class. There was no significant difference in average final grades when students selected the assignment weights and when I set the weightings as I had done in the previous year.

In general, higher-achieving students rated the experience more positively than did the lower-achieving students. It may be that higher-achieving students have a better sense of their academic strengths. It is also possible that their locus of control is more internal, which contributes positively to learning.

This research was conducted with graduating seniors, which probably influenced the outcome. Seniors have had more time in college to assess their academic performance in terms of knowing which assignments work well for them. First- and second-year students, even high-achieving ones, may not be able to handle this approach as well.

Other research documents that students often expect grades much higher than they ultimately earn. This is particularly true of low-achieving students, who may be less motivated when the teacher sets the grade weights.

Giving students more control over grading at the outset by allowing them to select the percentage value of each assignment may increase their motivation. Doing so does not jeopardize how well they do in the course, or at least it didn't in my course.

Reprinted from *The Teaching Professor*, 23.7 (2009): 2.

Should Student Effort Count?

By Maryellen Weimer, Penn State-Berks, Pennsylvania

We've all had conversations with students who want effort counted in their grade. "But I tried so hard . . . I studied for hours . . . I am really working in this course." The question is, should effort count?

Less commonly asked, however, is whether it should count in both directions. Students want effort to count when they try hard but their performance doesn't show it. But what about when an excellent performance results without much effort? Should this lack of effort lower the grade? Beyond these theoretical questions are the pragmatic ones: Can effort be measured fairly, objectively? If so, what criteria are used to assess it?

Using survey research, a faculty team explored these questions. Their study builds on earlier work by J.B. Adams, and some of their findings replicated those reported earlier. Faculty respondents in the Adams study reported that in a situation where student effort was high but performance was low, approximately 17 percent of the grade should be ascribed to effort.

Students in that study thought that in those circumstances 38 percent of the grade should be based on effort. In this study, the percentages were similar. Faculty thought 13 percent of the grade should be given for effort and students thought 39 percent was appropriate. A bit surprising, though, was the fact that students were more willing than faculty to penalize students when their effort was low but the performance was high.

These overall averages were looked at more specifically in terms of the type of course: should effort count more or less in a required general education course, a general education elective, a required course in the major, an elective in the major, a minor requirement, or a medical course? Faculty thought the kind of course did not make a difference. Effort should count the same regardless of the course. Students reported that course type should make a difference.

The survey also included some interesting questions that pertained to study habits, such as "For a 3-credit course, how many hours of studying a week would indicate outstanding performance?" Students said 6.73 hours (SD 4.41), and faculty said 8.53 hours (SD 3.72). They also asked about typical study patterns—cramming, weekly study and review, or daily studying. Faculty estimated that 68 percent of the students studied by mostly cramming for exams. Students chose cramming as the typical study pattern 53 percent of the time.

That difference is significant. Perhaps more important is that cramming remains a common approach to study for many students much of the time. Finally, students estimated that on average students spend 14.10 hours a week studying. Faculty estimated weekly student study time at 19.10 hours. That's another significant difference.

As for measuring effort, both students and faculty agreed that it is a difficult construct to measure. Can it be measured by class attendance? Regular participation in class? Self-reports? Both faculty and students agreed that effort is best measured by performance on assigned work. If the student is working hard, that will be seen in the work they produce and on their exam performance. Both agreed that the least accurate measure of effort are those self-reports.

"These results suggest that students and faculty may benefit from communication about grading procedures and policies, as well as [from] a frank discussion regarding what faculty consider to be 'outstanding effort' in a class. Students likely do not know what workload is appropriate for college-level courses and often struggle because they do not know how to direct their effort." (p. 15)

Reference: Zinn, T.E., Magnotti, J.F., Marchuk, K., Schultz, B.S., Luther, A., and Varfolomeeva, V. (2011). "Does effort still count? More on what makes the grade." *Teaching of Psychology*, 38 (1), 10–15.

Entitled: Ways to Respond to Students Who Think They Are

By Maryellen Weimer, Penn State-Berks, Pennsylvania

Student entitlement can be defined academically: "a self-centered disposition characterized by a general disregard for traditional faculty relationship boundaries and authority" (p. 198), or it can be described more functionally: "a sense that they [students] deserve what they want because they want it and want it now." (p. 197)

Examples illustrate what many faculty have experienced with these students: complaints because a 2:00 a.m. email was not answered before an 8:00 a.m. class; wanting effort to count for points and credit ("But I tried, I really tried to find those references"); or requests to be exempted from requirements (such as course prerequisites) because "I don't need that course."

Students who arrive in college with this sense of entitlement are not a majority, and any consideration of how to respond to these students needs to be measured against how those responses will affect the learning environment for other students. The authors of a well-referenced article on student entitlement estimate that fewer than 10 percent of students fall into this category, but they point out that these students tend to require "a far greater proportion" of a faculty member's time and energy.

The article includes a useful discussion of the bases for this sense of entitlement. The authors see it as resulting from cultural norms and expectations, specifically the consumer mentality that characterizes how students orient to college. It's no longer about intellectual experiences; a college degree is now seen as a "ticket" to a better job.

Universities must now compete for students, and they do so by "selling" a college experience that comes with fancier living accommodations, extensive choices for food, 24-hour fitness centers, and so on. They also see grade inflation as contributing to students' senses of entitlement. Show up and do the work even at a minimal level and you can expect to get a B. And finally they discuss generational differences and document an increase in levels of narcissism among college students today.

The authors suggest six strategies for responding to students with a sense of entitlement. Each is briefly highlighted here, with many more details appearing in the article.

Make expectations explicit. The best place to begin doing this is on the syllabus. The authors recommend using grading rubrics that break assignments into parts and then designate a value for each component. Rubrics make expectations clear, but they also help instructors explain grading decisions to students. They can be used to structure those conversations.

Give students something to lose by negotiating. Entitled students often ask for grade changes or to have their work reevaluated. There is also some evidence that when students argue for more points with professors, they typically get some. What the authors recommend is that faculty agree to reevaluate work but that reassessment may result in the grade being raised or the grade being lowered (or it may stay the same).

Entitled students ask for reevaluations of their work because they have nothing to lose. This strategy introduces the possibility that there might be something lost, and this gives students pause before making the request.

Provide examples of "excellent" work. Many college students, especially beginning ones, do not have an accurate sense of the quality of their work. It may well be that they worked harder on this paper than on any other they've ever written, but it still may be well below college standards. Examples can be used to show students the differences between what they have done and what happens in an A paper.

If these "excellent" examples are provided after students have done the assignment, this prevents students from attempting to copy the format without developing their own frameworks.

Ask students to make the case first in writing. If students believe their works merits more points than have been awarded, don't have a discussion with them about that until they have explained why in writing. This helps defuse the emotion that often accompanies these exchanges, and it enables both the student and faculty member to prepare for the conversation.

Re-socialize students and faculty. "Explain your philosophy of teaching and learning and your focus on student responsibility. ... Socialize students into assuming responsibility for their own efforts and their own learning so that they are less likely to blame you for any shortcomings." (p. 202) That's re-socializing students—for faculty, the authors recommend attempting to understand today's college students better.

That doesn't mean accepting behavior that compromises the educational enterprise, but it does mean coming to grips with who these students are.

Institutional responses. The authors believe that institutional climate plays a role in determining how students behave and that certain climates diminish the amount of entitlement students may feel. They use rigorous first-year seminars as an example of how some institutions establish intellectual expectations for students.

The authors conclude by reiterating that this sense of entitlement is not characteristic of all college students. When faculty consider strategies that respond to entitlement, they must do so with an eye toward the learning needs of those students who come to college expecting their courses to be work and their thinking to be challenged.

Reference: Lippmann, S., Bulanda, R.E., and Wagenaar, T.C. (2009). "Student entitlement: Issues and strategies for confronting entitlement in the classroom and beyond." *College Teaching,* 57 (4), 197–203.

Reprinted from *The Teaching Professor,* 24.7 (2010): 8.

The Final (Office) Hours

By Gary R. Hafer, Lycoming College, Pennsylvania

The final portfolio of student work (be it writings, drawings, or a collection of different kinds of work) presents the instructor with a conundrum. As the culmination of student work, it needs to be submitted at the end of the course, but feedback opportunities then are severely limited. Those of us who use portfolio assignments do provide feedback at multiple points throughout the semester, but when the portfolio is completed, the course has ended and this final version cannot be discussed with students.

Worse than that, for years I cringed as I saw the graded portfolios accumulate outside my office. Some were never picked up.

Interested in a better alternative, I initiated "the final hour," an open office hour for any student interested in conversing about his/her graded portfolio. The procedure is straightforward. As with my previous practice, students have until Monday noon during final examination week to submit their portfolios.

I've seen the original and revised pieces in the portfolios throughout the semester and during a "trial run" conference where I give them a ballpark grade of where the portfolio is presently situated. This enables me to read the final product quickly, usually finishing by Tuesday evening, after which I send out an email with a grade report. In the email header, I announce first: "Questions? Discussion? Complaints? FINAL OPEN OFFICE HOURS, Wednesday 10–12." The email note contains all the details and the final grade, although I typically don't submit final grades to the registrar until after that conference time; I'm open to students' input.

Final conference attendance varies, and so do the reasons why students decide to drop by. Some want to chat, just as they do with me before class starts. Some others want to see what I liked, delighted that their final grade is higher than they expected. Still others solicit empathy; I listen to them reason through their disappointment, which helps me understand the decisions they made—or did not make—in revision.

They tell me this time is comforting to them too. One student just wanted to tell me "how hard it was to even earn a D." I find there are learning opportunities during this last conference as students and I make our way through their portfolios and I share my reactions to them.

The final conference also helps me. It makes me a more careful final grader because, whether a student attends the final office hour or not, I may have to face him or her and defend my decision. That influence is not debilitating; rather, it is mightily persuasive in keeping me centered on making my evaluation "honest." As Peter Elbow notes in his book *Everyone Can Write* (p. 357), the high-stakes response is a "critical" one that "is more likely to misfire or do harm because of how it is received—even if it is sound … "

The final office hour gives me an opportunity to listen and to see how that graded message is received—a rare opportunity to hear a student's side after the final portfolio is graded. The student controls the final hour with questions and complaints, all of which I respond to. I discover, however, that I do far more listening than talking.

The final hour also provides a space for quick resolution. Without it, grade debate can linger on. One semester I had a student and his father debating whether to appeal the final portfolio grade, which for the student meant the final course grade; the email discussions went back and forth between the freshman dean and the student's parent, with me as the bystander, supplying information and commentary along the way only to the dean.

It was a bizarre way to look at my own grading, defending it in the role of a third party. Since implementing the final hour, I've avoided such scenarios.

Although I'm responsible for the academic integrity of the course, I also understand that I need to keep communication open, even after students have finished the course. Therefore, I'm not averse to changing a grade as a result of the final conference. Yet, I never have and no student has asked me to do so.

Instead, that final hour provides something different: an exchange and a shared understanding that can come only after a final piece of work is discussed. The worst that has ever come out of the final hour is to have students agree to disagree, parting without acrimony. The stack of unclaimed portfolios outside my office is significantly smaller now. That reason alone justifies the final hour opportunity.

Reprinted from *The Teaching Professor,* 26.3 (2012): 1.

Why Don't Students Use Teacher Feedback to Improve?

By Maryellen Weimer, Penn State-Berks, Pennsylvania

Here's the conclusion of a small but intriguing study. Its findings reveal "only limited support for the idea that students actually do respond to feedback and make changes in a subsequent piece of assessable work consistent with the intentions that underlay the provided feedback." (p. 577)

And what's the evidence that supports this conclusion? A cohort of 51 undergraduate social work students (some taking the course online and some on campus) wrote two 1,750-word essays six weeks apart. They were given a choice of topics: four for the first essay and five for the second. The format and grading criteria for both essays were the same and were given to students with opportunities to discuss and ask questions prior to preparation of the essays.

Feedback on the first essay focused on areas where the student could make improvements. Potential evaluator bias was controlled via several mechanisms. Grades for both essays were within four points of each other for 66.7 percent of the cohort. Close to 16 percent of the students showed substantial improvement, and a bit more than 17 percent showed a substantial decline in performance.

The researcher admits with some candor, "Like many academics, the author's first instinct was to blame the students for their apparent disregard for the feedback they were given." (p. 577) And students are not blameless. She includes citations from other research documenting that students spend little time reading the instructor-provided feedback.

In one study 39 percent of the students indicated they spent five minutes or less reading the feedback. A total of 81 percent spent 15 minutes or less reading feedback. She wonders whether students are so focused on just getting the second assignment done that they don't see the point of the feedback and have no interest in understanding or trying to use it.

Maybe they are satisfied with the grade on the first assignment and figure that if they do the second one the same way, they'll do just as well. They aren't thinking about what they might learn if they tried to respond to the feedback.

"For academics, a less comfortable option than blaming students for their apparent ignoring of feedback is to critically reflect on their own practices." (p. 578) She goes on to explain, "Providing information prior to an assignment regarding the criteria for assessment, followed up by written feedback on the completed assignment, frequently represents a series of unilateral pronouncements by assessors rather than a dialogue with students." (p. 578)

This is another example of teaching by telling¬—of expecting students to learn by listening as opposed to learning by discovering and doing.

She also wonders whether students receive consistent feedback across the collection of courses they take during a semester. Are all their professors identifying the same problems and recommending the same areas for improvement?

Chances are good they aren't. If the messages are mixed, even contradictory, that can be confusing to the student and could explain the frequent but annoying query, "What do you want on this paper?" If the messages are multiple, that may result in an overwhelming amount of feedback, so the student copes by ignoring some or all of it.

This study is small, but it does raise a number of interesting questions that probe more deeply into the role of teacher feedback and improved student performance. It challenges us to consider both student and teacher actions that might diminish the role of feedback in promoting learning and improving performance.

Reference: Crisp, B.R. (2007). "Is it worth the effort? How feedback influences students' subsequent submission of assessable work." *Assessment & Evaluation in Higher Education*, 32 (5), 571–581.

Reprinted from *The Teaching Professor,* 26.4 (2012): 2.

Using Post-test Analysis to Help Students See Correlation between Effort and Performance

By Maryellen Weimer, Penn State-Berks, Pennsylvania

One of the student engagement techniques (SETs) described in Elizabeth F. Barkley's new book on student engagement (see a review of the book elsewhere in this issue) has students predicting and reflecting on their exam preparation and performance. It's a technique that helps students see the correlation between their efforts and their exam scores, as well as one that helps them assess the effectiveness of the study strategies they use.

Here's how the activity works. After students have finished the exam but before submitting it, they complete a short post-test analysis questionnaire—you may need to state that you won't accept the exam unless the analysis sheet is attached. Barkley suggests having students respond to items such as:

- Predict your exam score.
- Rate your effort in studying for the exam on a scale of 1 (lowest) to 10 (highest).
- List the specific learning strategies you used to study for the exam. (Did you make flash cards to help you memorize definitions? Rewrite your notes? Create outlines of assigned readings? Discuss the readings with other students?)
- Identify what you found easiest and most difficult about the exam, and explain why.

After the exam has been graded and returned, students do a second analysis—you might want to not record the exam scores until students complete the second analysis, or you might want to offer some bonus points to those students who complete both analyses thoughtfully and carefully. Here are some of the suggested items for this second analysis:

- Describe your emotional response to your exam score. (Surprised? Disappointed? Relieved? Pleased?)
- Compare your actual score with your predicted score, and comment on how well or poorly you predicted your score.
- Identify where each question came from (in-class material, book material, online resources) and then calculate the percentage of questions missed in each of the categories. What do these percentages tell you?
- Reflect on the strategies you used for studying for this exam and the amount of time you devoted to study. Describe any changes you plan to make in your approach to studying for the next exam.
- Do you have any suggestions for how I or your classmates could help you better prepare for the next exam?
- Based on your performance on this exam, set one goal for the next exam. Make the goal specific and concrete (e.g., "I plan to get at least 75 percent of the questions from the reading materials correct.").

An activity like this is most beneficial if it's completed early in the course so that students can act on what they have learned. Although the advantages of such an activity may be perfectly obvious to the teacher, don't assume that students will automatically see the value of this kind of analysis.

Introduce the activity with a discussion of things students can do to improve their exam performance in this (and other) course(s). If students do the activity for more than one exam, you might want to add an item that has them track their performance across the exams, asking to what they attribute their improvement (or lack thereof). Barkley points out that this activity is easily adaptable to other kinds of assignments, such as written work or projects.

Reference: Barkley, E.F. *Student Engagement Techniques: A Handbook for College Faculty.* San Francisco: Jossey-Bass, 2009, 336–339.

Reprinted from *The Teaching Professor,* 23.10 (2009): 1.

About the Editor and Contributors

About Maryellen Weimer, Ph.D.

Maryellen Weimer, Ph.D., created *The Teaching Professor* newsletter in 1987 and is its editor. She is professor emerita of Teaching and Learning at Penn State Berks and won Penn State's Milton S. Eisenhower award for distinguished teaching in 2005. Dr. Weimer is the author of several books, including: *Learner-Centered Teaching: Five Key Changes to Practice* (Jossey-Bass, 2013), *Inspired College Teaching: A Career-Long Resource for Professional Growth* (Jossey-Bass, 2010), *Enhancing Scholarly Work on Teaching* and *Learning: Professional Literature that Makes a Difference* (Jossey-Bass, 2006).

About Barbara E. Walvoord, Ph.D.

Barbara E. Walvoord, Ph.D., author of the foreword for this e-book, is professor emerita at the University of Notre Dame, Indiana. Dr. Walvoord has written and edited many books, including *Effective Grading: A Tool for Learning and Assessment in College* (2nd ed., Jossey-Bass, 2010) and *Assessment Clear and Simple: A Practical Guide for Institutions, Departments, and General Education* (2nd ed., Jossey-Bass, 2010). Dr. Walvoord is the founding director of four nationally recognized faculty-development programs. She has consulted with more than 350 campuses on assessment, teaching and learning, and writing across the curriculum.

Contributors

Jan D. Andersen, California State University, Sacramento, CA
Karinda Barrett, Tallahassee Community College, FL
Matt Birkenhauer, Northern Kentucky University, KY
Deborah Bracke, Augustana College, IL
Kevin Brown, Lee University, TN
Adam Chapnick, University of Toronto, Canada
Paul T. Corrigan, Southeastern University, FL
Ed Cunliff, University of Central Oklahoma
Audrey L. Deterding, Indiana University Southeast, IN
Kathy Gehr, College of Charleston, SC
Francine S. Glazer, Kean University, NJ
Gary R. Hafer, Lycoming College, PA
Frances S. Johnson, Rowan University, NJ
Denise D. Knight, SUNY Cortland, NY

Bill Latham, US Army Command and General Staff College, Fort Leavenworth, KS
Anna H. Lathrop, Brock University, Ontario, Canada
Jerry Reed, Valencia Community College, Orlando, FL, and Nancy Small Reed, FL
Brian A. Vander Schee, Aurora University, IL
John Sturtridge, Cambrian College, Ontario, Canada
Susan M. Taylor, Andrew University, MI
Scott Warnock, Penn State Berks, PA
Maryellen Weimer, Penn State Berks, PA

Additional Resources

If you enjoyed this e-book, *The Teaching Professor* has additional resources for you:

E-book

Teaching Strategies for the College Classroom: A Collection of Faculty Articles (http://amzn.to/Yas3NE)

This e-book contains a practical, classroom-tested "tool kit" for faculty members who would like to develop their teaching practice. The 35 articles are written by college faculty for college faculty. They contain concrete pedagogical strategies that have been tested in the authors' classrooms and together form a handbook of classroom strategies.

Free Resources

- Subscribe to *Faculty Focus (facultyfocus.com)* — An e-newsletter on effective teaching strategies for the college classroom, featuring a weekly blog post from Maryellen Weimer, Ph.D.
- Join *The Teaching Professor*'s LinkedIn Group *(http://linkd.in/1496hsq)*
- Like *The Teaching Professor* on Facebook *(facebook.com/TeachingProfessor)*
- Follow *The Teaching Professor* on Twitter *(@teachprof)*

Paid Resources

The Teaching Professor **Newsletter** *(teachingprofessor.com/newsletter)*
All articles in this e-book are from past editions of this newsletter. Published ten times a year, *The Teaching Professor* newsletter features ideas, insights, and best pedagogical practices written for and by educators who are passionate about teaching. Edited by Maryellen Weimer, Ph.D.

The Teaching Professor **Conference** *(teachingprofessor.com/conferences)*
This annual event provides an opportunity to learn effective pedagogical techniques, hear from leading teaching experts, and interact with colleagues committed to teaching and learning excellence.

(Continued on page 106)

The Teaching Professor Technology Conference
(teachingprofessor.com/conferences)
This conference examines the technologies that are changing the way
teachers teach and students learn, while giving special emphasis to the
pedagogically effective ways you can harness these new technologies in your
courses and on your campus.

The Teaching Professor Workshops *(teachingprofessor.com/workshops)*
These are two-day "hands-on" learning events. At the end of the
workshop, you will leave with a product or process that you can implement
immediately. Topics include: learner-centered course design, grading, and
blended learning.

***

Made in the USA
Lexington, KY
13 November 2014